Las Crosses

An Unwavering Journey to a New Life in America

Apple An

Voices Heard Publishing, LLC

AWARDS

Finalist for the "Women's Non-Fiction" and "Multicultural Non-Fiction" awards at The 2023 IAN Book of the Year Awards

PRAISE FOR THE AUTHOR

Endorsements from Published Authors

"*A story of opportunity, bravery and self-invention that's as suspenseful and inspiring as it is quintessentially Amer-*

ican." – **Jonathan Dee**, finalist for the Pulitzer Prize for Fiction

"It is an enjoyable and essential read on cultural contrast from a historical era." - **Ginnah Howard**, author of I'm Sick of This Already, Rope & Bone, Night Navigation, and Doing Time Outside

"An's writing powerfully depicts scenes, characters, and emotions with a bit of comedy. This is undoubtedly an important topical work for 2020s America." - **Cate McGowan**, author of These Lowly Objects and True Places Never Are

"An inspiring story of resilience, hope and joyful curiosity, even in the face of uncertainty and difficulty. Uplifting!" – **Diane Pienta**, author of Be the Magic

"An engrossing and well-written memoir with a subtle humor." – **Bob Gates**, author of Extreme Measures, Nothing to Give, Creation Myths, Messages to Myself, InSight, among others.

Selected Review Excerpts on Writing

"The author's storytelling skillfully portrays Apple's voice, evoking emotions and chuckles." – **Steven Barr**

"A profound and epic journey, told with such preternatural humility, gentle humor, and the intrepid innocence and grace. A shade of Lewis Carroll in the unfolding." – **Mark Wells**

"A very vivid picture of the cultural clash. Lighthearted, captivating, and heartwarming, full of unexpected twists with an ending that is quite satisfying!" – **Kevin Boyle**

"Fast-paced, engaging, and filled with unexpected twists, keeping me captivated until the satisfying ending. The cultural contrast, historical events, and vivid descriptions make it an educational and insightful read." – **Pierre Camille**

"I feel like I watched the movie and not just read the book. The pictures add a personal touch." – **Maria Leonova**

"A well-written, compelling journey! So authentic and really engaging. Highly recommend it, even for people like me who don't typically read memoirs. I wanted to see this as a movie!" - **Brad Witbeck**

"This story is like a majestic odyssey, narrated with a humility that could make even the most egotistical peacock blush. It's filled with humor so gentle that it could tame *a wild lion, and the fearless innocence and elegance of Apple, a young lady who embraces every daunting adventure and nerve-wracking encounter with the grace of a ballerina. It's like stepping into An's shoes and seeing life through her fabulous perspective. Well, it seems like not all memoirs got the memo on how to be engaging, but this one definitely nailed it! The content was so captivating that it had me hooked like a fish on a line, unable to escape its literary lure. Highly recommended!"* – **Miguyver**

On Content

"Real life and a major life change, through the eyes of a valuable human being with a good heart. Kudos for a well-written journal." - **Dave Campbell**

"An inspiring tale for a 1st generation like myself." - **Tom Jones**

"Nuggets for establishing and embracing life like curiosity, fearlessness, relationship management, thankfulness, and appreciation. They can lead to a full and exciting life anywhere!" – **James Emery**

"Through her eyes, we witness the challenges and triumphs of a woman fearlessly navigating unfamiliar territories and embracing every new experience that comes her way. It lies in its ability to infuse ordinary moments with extraordinary significance. Apple's voyage becomes a bridge between East and West, tradition and modernity, and the lessons she learns along the way are universal in their appeal. Her narrative resonates deeply, serving as a testament to the power of perseverance and the beauty of embracing diversity." - **Lester W.**

"What a great find – This is such an interesting book to understand how cultures differ and how humans are much more similar to each other than it is commonly believed. This is a book about challenges, courage, and overcoming difficulties. I have an enormous respect for this author and what she has created—pure literary art. Great book." – **D. Dutra**

On Emotions and Effects

"This hidden gem of a memoir will lift your spirits and touch your heart. Read it soon, and share it with others!" - **Fran Green**

"A fantastic book that left me feeling inspired and motivated. The book has defi-

nitely left a lasting impression on me, and I would highly recommend it to anyone looking for a powerful and uplifting read. The young woman in the story serves as an amazing role model for women everywhere, encouraging us to follow our hearts, heads, and spirits and pursue our dreams with passion and purpose." - **Igor Kirko**

"From the first page, this book grabs you and holds you in thrall with its raw and moving story. This story will make you feel a wide range of emotions that will grab you and stir your soul for a long time. You'll want to read this book again and again because of how deep the story is and how much of an effect it has." - **Robbie Jones**

"I loved reading about her. It's like she's a superhero in real life! If you want to read a story about never giving up and follow-

ing your dreams, this book is excellent." - **Isabella Garcia**

"The story often made me think, stop, and take the time to smell the roses. An's true story telling is so fragrant." - **Jill Shoob**

"Makes you appreciate the simple things." - **Janessa Werhane**

"You will make a wonderful, warm, determined new friend with this story. This book made me smile many times." - **Sarah Wiles**

On Future Stories

"I hope that there's more to come." - **Charles Martin Cosgriff**

"I cannot wait for the sequel, what I'm sure will be another walk in the park, another bouquet." - **Jill Shoob**

"Such a great read, waiting for the next book to see the journey continue in Austin!"
- T. Owla

"I was absolutely captivated by this candid glimpse into the life of a Chinese immigrant. I am really looking forward to reading other books about this author's phenomenal life."
- Feather Chelle

"I'm eager for her to write how her life progressed after her move to Austin Texas. I find myself very invested." **- Shaden Elkhatib**

"The book's ending brings a comforting closure, yet an invitation lingers to delve deeper into Apple's world. As Apple navigates cultural shifts, readers find themselves contemplating their own perspectives. The story's humility and charm captivate, leaving a desire to know more about the enchanting Apple An." – **Steven Barr**

"It's worth noting that this is Apple's debut work, and its significance cannot be understated as it marks a pivotal point in her life, serving as the steppingstone from which she launched her literary exploration of the stories that shaped her life before and after the events depicted here." - **Lester W.**

Copyright

Copyright © 2023 by Voices Heard Publishing, LLC
All right reserved.
This work may not be copied, reproduced, or translated in whole or in part without the written permission of the publisher, except for brief excerpts in connection with reviews or scholarly analysis.
This is a work of nonfiction. Events and experiences detailed herein are all true and have been faithfully portrayed as the author has remembered them to the

best of her ability. To protect the privacy and anonymity of the people involved, some names and identities have been changed.

ISBN:
978-1-958900-01-7 (RP paperback)
978-1-958900-00-0 (RP hardcover)
978-1-958900-06-2 (LP paperback)
978-1-958900-05-5 (LP hardcover)
978-1-958900-02-4 (eBook)
ASIN B0C3F54CW9 (audiobook)

Cover design: Melody Gan
Artwork rendering: Tony Li & GetCovers.com

4th Regular Printing
1st Large Printing
December 2023

DEDICATION

for the children under my wings who wouldn't exist without this transition

Contents

Acknowled-gments	XIX
Preface	XXI
1. Arrival	1
2. Housing	30
3. Friends from the Past	53
4. My Name is Apple	64
5. Yolanda	73
6. First TV Set	96
7. Dropped-Noodle Soup	105
8. The Wheels	120

9.	Driving to the West	129
10.	Movies and Music	156
11.	Summer Jobs	178
12.	Moving on	198
13.	Dear Reader	217
14.	About the Author	219

Acknowledgments

I am deeply grateful to everyone who helped make this book happen. The children I raised and cared for inspired me to write about my life. Georgia P. helped me in ways she wouldn't be able to imagine. My writing buddies, Amy J., Carol D., D'Arcy F., Dan C., Donna M., Gwendolyn D., Kim B., Pam B., Pam C., and Susan W., provided constructive feedback on early drafts and cheered me on to write honestly, fearlessly, and for a broader audience than I initially planned. I thank my editor Elisabeth B. for her insightful suggestions. I value Melody G. and Tony L. for their creative artistic contributions. Finally, my special thanks go to Jim E., who was more than a reader, an editor, and an admirer.

Preface

Las Cruces (/lɑːsˈkrusɪs/; Spanish: [las ˈkruses] "the crosses") is the second-largest city in the U.S. state of New Mexico. In 1990, it had a population of 62,648.

1
ARRIVAL

I stepped out of the El Paso airport and into the bright afternoon of December 15th, 1989. The sky was a deep shade of blue that I had never seen before. The sun shone behind the tall trees. *Are they palm trees?* I wondered and took a deep breath. *Such fresh air, no smokiness like the air in Beijing.* I took another deep inhale, this time with a wide-open mouth, and exhaled slowly. *Finally!*

My travel companion Qin and I were excited, but for different reasons. We had first met at the U.S. Embassy in Beijing to get our visas. We learned that we were both going to the same city—Las Cruces, New Mexico—for the spring semester. Qin was to join her husband, who had come one semester earlier as a doctoral student in the same department where I would be studying. How coincidental, considering that Las Cruces was quite an unknown place in the U.S. (as I would later learn). This might have been just another sign that my destiny was to be in America now.

Our excitement made us forget the fatigue, frustration, and anxiety we'd experienced earlier that morning. After a thirteen-hour flight from Beijing, our cross-Pacific airplane had landed in Los Angeles. There, we inched forward in one of several long lines of multiracial visitors and were interrogated by stone-faced customs officers. Qin was lucky and passed the luggage checkpoint without trouble. I was horrified to watch an officer dismantle my two packed suitcases. I struggled for a long time to repack the bags with no success. Sweating heavily even in the gigantic, air-conditioned building and worried that we might miss our connecting flight, I took out some clothes and wrapped them in a bedsheet to carry with me. I could finally zip up the suitcases and pushed them to the connecting luggage area. Despite being hungry and thirsty, we did not dare take the time to stop anywhere. The airport was dazzlingly confusing. We had to speak our broken English to ask people in uniforms for directions. We attempted to make sense of the unfamiliar signs. We made wrong turns several times. Eventually, we found the right terminal in time to get on the flight to El Paso, the closest airport to Las Cruces. *It's okay. I've encountered worse. These are all just necessary steps toward my destination,* I told myself.

In contrast, the El Paso airport was much smaller and easier to navigate. Almost no time after landing, we were already outside.

Qin shrieked and left my side. I saw her running to the arms of a young man with a full head of black hair. Next to him was a middle-aged Caucasian man. *He must be Dr. Davidson, my new advisor.*

Dr. Davidson was the first American I had ever interacted with—and it had been through snail mail. I learned about New Mexico State University from *Peterson's Guide*, an annual publication of multiple volumes, each page crammed with about one thousand tiny words detailing U.S. universities, majors, and professors. At that time, one could only find *Peterson's Guide* in a comprehensive library such as the National Library in Beijing.

The Tiananmen protest and the aftermath in June 1989 prompted me to send applications to American universities that summer, sooner than planned. I was thrilled when, within less than a month, I received an acceptance letter signed by Dr. Davidson notifying me that I was to start in the spring semester. Until then, all other people I had known, who had attended American universities, started in the fall semester. Dr. Davidson also signed a financial-aid letter offering me a teaching assistantship to be financially self-sufficient, a critical criterion for getting an American visa. When I needed confirmation to get through the challenging process of applying for my passport, Dr. responded immediately with a letter that reached me within three days.

From that moment on, there was only one direction for me to go—I quit my job, got rid of my belongings, and sealed my hukou, the citizenship proof required to live in China. I became non-existent. Dr. Davidson was a key player in bringing me to the U.S. at this almost impossible time.

For some reason, I had an image of him being tall and heavy, with a commanding air and scholarly glasses, and dressed formally. I was surprised to see him fit, with a slim medium build, and casually dressed in a polo shirt and khaki pants. He was in his 50s, had gray hair balding at the top, and a clean-shaven face. His large gray eyes were kind, humble, and deep.

Dr. Davidson grinned when he recognized me. Then, he walked quickly toward me, said, "Welcome," and gave me a big bear hug.

I was startled by his arms around me. With no time to think, I awkwardly turned my face away, feeling uncomfortable. I couldn't remember getting a big hug like that from anyone, not even my mom. Immediately, I regretted turning away. *I hope Dr. Davidson is not offended*. I faced him with an apologetic smile.

After loading all the luggage into the trunk of a Jeep, Qin and her husband climbed into the back seat. Dr. Davidson opened the passenger's door for me.

"It'll be a 45-minute drive from the airport to Las Cruces," he said with a smile.

This was the first car ride I ever had in the U.S. I liked the Jeep immediately for its sand color, square-cornered shape, and high-above-the-ground feeling. Of course, the fact that Dr. Davidson drove a Jeep raised its standing highly in my mind. Sitting in the passenger seat, I stretched my neck, looking up and around.

The sky seemed so low; the clouds were hanging at an almost reachable height and moving quickly. *Why's that?* The sky in China had always seemed unreachable, so we had the saying, "as high as the sky." Gradually I realized that there were no tall buildings along our route. There was virtually nothing but desert, with bushes and utility poles on both sides of the road.

Just as I was puzzling over what I saw and didn't see, Dr. Davidson stopped the car at an intersection, waited for a car from another direction to go, then continued.

I looked around—no traffic lights.

What just happened? Cars wait for other cars? Never seen that in China before. Where are the traffic lights?

Over the next 20 minutes or so, I did not see a single traffic light. I also noticed only a few cars passing in the opposite direction.

Hmmm. This is all very strange. Where am I? Am I dreaming? Is this America? I turned my head to the left—Dr. Davidson gave me a big smile. I looked back and saw Qin and her husband holding each other in the back seat as if the rest of the world didn't exist. I pinched my leg and felt the pain. Whatever this was, it was so drastically different from the images I had seen in the videos about the U.S.: tall skyscrapers next to each other under the high sky, multi-lane roads filled with fancy cars, traffic lights at busy intersections, and large colorful billboards on the sides of the streets.

It did not help my confusion when my jet lag kicked in, and my head felt heavy. I drifted into unconsciousness unknowingly.

The car's stopping, followed by someone saying, "Thank you, see you later," woke me up. Qin and her husband were being dropped off at their apartment. It was dark outside.

Dr. Davidson got back into the car, fastened his seat belt, then turned to me, "How are you doing?"

"Okay." I was embarrassed that I hadn't stayed awake during the drive.

"Have you ever seen any Christmas decorations?"

"Not really."

"How about I show you some Christmas lights next?"

"Okay." I was curious now.

We reached a neighborhood on top of a hill in a few minutes. In front of us, lined up on the ground, were mysterious and beautiful lights that made me think of candles the way they flickered, but they looked as if they were in large rectangle-shaped brown paper bags. These lights were spaced out from each other and formed patterns as they outlined the walkways or stretched out in different directions. Almost every house in the neighborhood had them. Some buildings and trees had smaller lights in various colors outlining the profiles or borders. This was a first for me. Christmas had begun to draw the attention of many Chinese people over the past few years. The previous Christmas Eve, a friend and I had ridden our bikes to visit two churches to check out what happened at such a time. We found people in gowns singing, their hands holding a big book. But there were no holiday decorations.

"How do you like the lights?" Dr. Davidson asked.

"Very much. They're unique and beautiful."

"I'm glad you like them. Here comes my house."

Dr. Davidson pulled into a driveway and parked the car. Lights surrounded his house, too, with a clear outline of the building and the neatly manicured yard. Dr. Davidson opened the front door and let me in. Two people immediately came to the door.

"This is my son Walter. He is a college student. And this is my daughter Diana, a graduate student. They're home for their school break," Dr. Davidson said.

They smiled at me and extended their hands politely for a handshake. That was a relief—I didn't know how I would react if they were to give me hugs.

My luggage was rolled into the guest room. Dr. Davidson let me rest a bit and then took the three of us to dinner.

Seated at a table, a waiter brought us four glasses of iced water. *Isn't it December now? Do people here drink iced water in the winter?* I'd never had iced water in winter while growing up. I couldn't recall iced water in summer either. We rarely had ice due to a lack of refrigerators. So most of us drank tea with boiled water all year long.

Walter and Diana headed to a long counter covered with a white tablecloth and many food trays.

Are people not served at the table? Are they picking their own food?

I turned to Dr. Davidson.

"This is a buffet dinner. We select whatever we would like to eat," Dr. Davidson said.

This was another first. There was no such thing in China at that time.

"Are you ready?" Dr. Davidson got up and smiled at me.

"Sure," I nodded and stood up.

Dr. Davidson led me to a long counter with no people around it. He passed me a big plate, then got one for himself. *What a big plate! For one person?* Back home, we would use such big plates to hold dishes to be shared by all the members at the table. I looked around. Small cups and plates were at the end of the counter, but no bowls like we used for rice or noodles. *Of course not—I never saw rice or noodles in the English training materials about America.*

"Those are for soups and desserts," Dr. Davidson said. *What are desserts?* I made a mental note to find out more.

Tray after tray of food was displayed. Some people in white coats constantly added more food or replaced the trays from the other side of the counter. I took a deep inhale. The food looked inviting, and my stomach started to rumble.

"Have you had these before?" Dr. Davidson asked, putting some items on his plate.

They looked like green vegetables, but I did not recognize them.

"Are they raw? Uncooked?" I looked around. *Are customers supposed to cook their own food?* We cooked all vegetables. Well, almost all—my sister and I would eat raw tomatoes and cucumbers after cleaning them thoroughly. We hardly ate raw greens because of worms or bugs.

"Yes, raw. These are lettuce, kale leaves, and broccoli. We eat them in a salad." Dr. Davidson put one leaf in his mouth.

The leafy greens I was familiar with were spinach and different types of cabbages. We also ate radish leaves when they were tender, but all those needed to be cooked with spices or salt. *Maybe these unfamiliar greens have their own flavors, like tomatoes or cucumbers?*

My puzzled face prompted Dr. Davidson to continue, "We put salad dressing on them to give them a certain flavor. Would you like to try some?"

"Okay." My favorite word now.

"How do you like this one?" He used a small spoon to dip into a yellowish sauce and put some on the edge of my plate.

"Wow, tasty but sour," I said.

"How about this one?" he asked, handing me a small spoon with pinkish sauce.

"Very sweet." I eyed the one next to it.

"Here, try them yourself." Dr. Davidson passed me a new spoon.

One was mild with just enough sourness and sweetness. I added it to my salad.

"Ah, so you like Italian," Dr. Davidson said.

"Maybe I'll try this white one too." I grabbed another spoon to reach the last dressing.

"That's Ranch."

"It's good too." I put Ranch on the other half of the salad plate.

The entire evening went by with Dr. Davidson patiently explaining everything and letting me smell or taste items before putting them on my plates.

I was overwhelmed by the variety and choices. Back home, I'd have one main dish and one side dish for each meal. We'd have several dishes at holidays or family gatherings, but you could still count them on the one hand. This first evening in the U.S., I had three plates of food. Despite my questions and uncertainties, I visited every counter and checked out every container or tray. I took just a tiny amount to have room to sample all of them. I discovered some tea bags and hot water. I found the warm soup intended for the cups. I learned what desserts were. I liked everything, as long as it was not super sweet.

I was determined to be open to anything new, regardless of how strange it might seem. After all, I had come across the globe to experience this new country I would now call home.

That first night, I slept in Dr. Davidson's guest room. Despite the 13-hour difference between Beijing and local time, I slept soundly.

When I got up the following day, Walter and Diana were out. Dr. Davidson was cooking cheese sandwiches. He let me taste the melted cheese and butter to ensure I liked them. I took a deep breath to take in the delicious scent. Growing up, I had never had any cheese or butter, even though my hometown in Inner Mongolia was famous for cows, sheep, and goats. Dairy products were considered luxuries. Few Chinese people of my generation or older were accustomed to eating them. Later I learned that the dried sour milk candies we sometimes got during the Spring Festivals were dairy products—*so maybe they should be considered some kind of cheese*? When I saw Dr. Davidson putting slices of bread on a flat pot, I said, "Uh oh" to myself. The bread was shown in many media I encountered when studying English and American culture, so I'd gotten the impression that it must be the leading food for Americans. To get ready to come to the U.S., I bought various types of bread from the campus cafeterias or local shops. But I disliked all of them. *Maybe the bread here tastes different? Remember, open your mind to everything.*

Indeed! The cheese sandwich Dr. Davidson made for my first breakfast in the U.S. was delicious!

After breakfast, I packed all my belongings and Dr. Davidson loaded them into his Jeep. Stepping outside his house, I looked around. It was a sunny day, with a blue sky and white clouds. I would eventually learn that Las Cruces had an average of 360 sunny days yearly! Dr. Davidson's yard was bigger than I had seen the night before. Green plants surrounded the house and extended along the driveway connected to the street. There was no fence or wall. I could see other homes. *It must be so safe here that there's no need for a fenced yard.* All the houses I had lived in had fences with gates that could be locked. Even so, kids in the neighborhood would sometimes climb the walls to get into our yards to either steal or vandalize. This neighborhood was formed along the street, with houses lined up and a great distance between them. Many of these single-story homes had beige-colored stone walls with rusty red flat roofs that made the buildings look like blocks. The landscapes surrounding them were beautifully shaped and laid out, although I only saw green plants, no flowers. *Why don't they add some colors by planting flowers?* Later, I learned that few flowers could survive the dry and hot climate.

Dr. Davidson patiently waited for me to get into the Jeep. We were to go to campus. Once we left the neighborhood, Dr.

Davidson drove on a single-lane gravel road surrounded by dirt and bushes. I turned my head to look back and saw a stream of yellow dust following the Jeep.

My first impression of the campus was its warmth, probably because most buildings were light yellow with rusty red roofs. It was such a good feeling on this sunny yet cold December day. Another impression was that everything seemed flat. The tallest buildings were three or four floors high.

Dr. Davidson parked the Jeep in a spacious parking lot in the center of the campus. Then, he guided me to the computer science building. Immediately, we met people in the hallways as we walked. Dr. Davidson introduced me to smiling face after smiling face, each of whom seemed to already know about me.

"Welcome!" "Glad you finally arrived." "So nice to meet you in person."

Addressing the puzzled look on my face, Dr. Davidson explained,

"Most people in the department—from faculty to administrative staff to students— know about you. This is a small department and we are very close to each other professionally and personally. Many of us reviewed your application. You impressed us with your credentials and achievements. We are all sympathetic to your situation back in China. Therefore, many strongly supported getting you here as soon as possible."

I was humbled and speechless. I had sensed strong invisible forces pulling me out of China. The people in this department must have been part of those forces.

Dr. Davidson introduced me to the department secretary, Tracy.

She stood up and gave me a firm handshake. "I'm so glad to meet you finally."

"Tracy is the one who sent out all the important documents I signed," said Dr. Davidson.

"Thank you for all your help," I said to Tracy.

Tracy gave me the email address she had already created for me, showed me the department mailbox, then led me to my office.

"You'll have to share this office with another doctoral student, although I'm told he's hardly ever here," Tracy said, almost apologetically.

I blinked in delight. Two huge windows made the room bright. A long desk in front of a window had a phone and a thin layer of dust. My officemate must have occupied the other long desk facing a wall and had a few books and stationery. A table between the two desks had a computer station on it. *That must be for all office mates to share.* A tall, empty bookshelf stood in the corner. A vast open space was in the middle, big enough for me to walk back and forth or dance around. This office was more spacious than any offices I had seen at Peking University (PKU) where I graduated and had worked as a junior faculty member before coming to America. Even our department chair's office was about one-third the size of this one. When I was teaching at PKU, regular faculty members had to share an office to meet students or hold small meetings. Here was my fancy workplace, the first ever I could call my own.

This armchair is very comfy. I can lower it by pressing this handle; now it's even more comfortable. I can put all my books there on the bookshelf. Or I could put them here on my big desk, as it would be easier to reach them. Why don't I get the ones in my luggage and put them here? Very good. More room for new ones. I need some writing pads, notebooks, and pens. I'd better create a shopping list. I should also log on to the computer and ensure my email works.

I descended into a wonderland without realizing the passing of time.

"Knock, knock"—a voice and a knocking sound came from my office door.

"Hi, come in," I responded.

A hairy man in his 40s stepped in and extended his hand.

"I'm Professor Parry. You'll be spending tonight at my place. Are you ready to go?"

"Hi. Glad to meet you. Dr. Davidson and I were at your office earlier, but you weren't in."

"I was teaching. You have met Jason and Lily already." He waved toward the door as the young couple poked in their smiling faces.

"Oh, hi again." I gestured to welcome them in. I vaguely remembered meeting them earlier, among several Chinese students Dr. Davidson had introduced me to.

"Are these your bags?" Professor Parry pointed to the two big suitcases and two smaller bags.

"Yes, they are." I zipped up my backpack.

Professor Parry pulled one suitcase and Jason dragged the second. Lily grabbed one smaller bag from the floor. We walked to the same parking lot Dr. Davidson had used and loaded my belongings into the trunk of a big car that could seat three people in front and three in the back.

I would spend the next three nights in Professor Parry's guest room.

2
Housing

Professor Parry was my official boss. My source of income was tied to being his teaching assistant for two undergraduate classes. About 5'10" with an average build, he had beautiful long and wavy black hair and the most enormous thick black beard I had ever seen, which left little visible skin on his face. During his classes, he would often use his left hand to fidget with the long beard in a pattern that made me predict the next moves with those fingers—it was so distracting that I'd missed some of his lectures. Sometimes he had his long hair tied up in a ponytail and sometimes kept it loose. I often saw his hair flowing around the hallway's corner before I saw him. He was just a very hairy man.

Professor Parry's neighborhood had single-story houses too, but it was very different from Dr. Davidson's. The buildings were closer to each other and set back from the road. They were mostly in various shades of gray and seemed newer but smaller. Although no fences existed, one could tell each property's boundaries.

Professor Parry parked the car and entered the main entrance. Jason took my bags to a side room. Lily carried hers and Jason's bags in. *Do Jason and Lily live here too?*

"Come on in," Professor Parry stood by the door and nodded at me.

Just as I entered the door, a giant, dark dog left Professor Parry's side and stood before me as if to hug me. He was almost my height!

"Ah!" I stepped back, panting in trepidation.

"Buddy, get back." Professor Parry held the dog and pushed him aside.

"Sorry. He doesn't usually do that. He must like you." Professor Parry's skin became red.

"Buddy is very friendly. Don't be afraid of him," said Lily.

Friendly? How friendly? Friendly as in not going to hurt me?

None of the dogs I had seen in China could be described as friendly. I did not know anyone who had dogs as pets. I had primarily seen street dogs that constantly searched for food or fought for food from humans. Thus, they were offensive toward humans. Or the humans made them offensive. A boy in our neighborhood was bitten in the calf when he tried to approach a dog and became permanently lame. We learned to stay as far away as possible from any dogs.

I inched inside, keeping my eyes on Buddy. I examined him thoroughly. He had shiny black-and-brown fur, a muscular build, a handsome face, and tall ears that stood up as if listening. His large eyes, to my surprise, were kind, warm, and intelligent. There was no aggression in them. He was as curious about me as I was about him.

Jason stood next to me and lifted Buddy's front right paw.

"Here, shake hands and you'll be friends," Jason nodded at me.

I paused for a moment. *Buddy's eyes are telling me that I can trust him.*

I shook "hands" with Buddy, and my guard came down eventually. I sat down on the end of a long sofa. Immediately, Buddy walked over and sat next to me. *Wow!* I was flattered.

"What kind of a dog is Buddy?" I asked.

"You mean breed? He's a German Shepherd," Professor Parry said.

The next few days, Buddy was around me whenever we met. I tried to put my hand on his back, and he let me. I moved my hand down his spine, and his tender eyes told me he enjoyed that. A few times, I stared into his eyes and wondered what he was thinking, and he looked right back, staring intensely into my eyes. Buddy was the first dog I ever got so close with. He left a significant imprint on me. *Someday, I'll have a German Shepherd just like Buddy.*

"You'll sleep next door in the guest room. Your bags are there already. I just checked to make sure clean towels are in the cabinet. Let me know if you need anything," Professor Parry said, bringing my attention back to human interactions.

The doorbell rang. Professor Parry went and came back with two flat, square-shaped boxes.

"Pizza, my favorite!" Lily exclaimed.

"You didn't like it when you first got here," Professor Parry said.

"That was two years ago. I've grown to like it very much," Lily said.

"You came two years ago?" I asked.

"Yes. Jason came first. He had to work in a restaurant to earn money to support himself. Professor Parry helped him a lot. Once the adoption was official, I came here and took English classes first, then enrolled in the Ph.D. program," said Lily.

"Adoption?" I asked again.

"Oh yeah. We are his adopted children. We call him Papa. He has never been married and has no children of his own. He is so kind to adopt us." Lily's gratitude was all over her face as she hugged Professor Parry, whose face went red again.

"I'm glad to have them. They help me occupy this big house. We carpool to school every day," Professor Parry said to me.

The guest room contained a bedroom and a bathroom. The bedroom's light gray tone gave it an elegant, soothing, and pleasant feel. The bed was huge and could easily sleep two people. I later learned it was a Queen-sized bed. A chest with many drawers and a large mirror was on one side of the room. On the other side was a wooden desk with two armchairs. At the ends of the armchairs were large plants. Finally, in the center of the room was a vast empty space.

An orange scent came out of the bathroom—Professor Parry had lit a candle for me. *How sweet and thoughtful.* I felt warmth in my heart. The bathroom had a similar color theme. There was a bathtub with a shower head. The middle of the room was, again, an ample empty space. *The entire guest place would make such a lovely home for a family of four.* I could not help but think of one of my former professors' living conditions in a one-room dormitory at PKU. Professor Fangyu's roommate in graduate school had moved out upon graduation, so he moved his family in from a city far away. A bunk bed for his son and daughter sat next to a double bed that he and his wife used. They worked, studied, ate in the room, and cooked in the hallway. Culture shock continued as I sensed a pattern: most places here, whether homes or offices, were generously spacious.

For a second night, I slept well. I felt almost no jet lag at all.

Breakfast awaited on the kitchen table when I greeted everyone in the morning. However, my oversensitive nose had not detected any evidence of cooking. Instead, in front of four large, empty bowls were four small bowls, each with half of a gigantic orange.

"Would you like some cereal?" Professor Parry lifted a wide rectangular box.

"What is it?" I examined the box and the contents of Jason's bowl.

"You'll like it." Lily smiled with confidence.

"Sure." I watched Professor Parry pour the flaky cereal into my bowl.

"Milk?" he asked, holding a tall rectangular bottle.

Cow milk was scarce when I was growing up. Because there were no refrigerators then, it was always stored in clear glass bottles at room temperature, so one could check whether the color was correct.

"Okay," I said. I wasn't a fan of milk, but I was curious and wanted to be polite.

"Grapefruit?" Professor Parry pointed to the bowl with the half orange.

"Grapefruit?" *Grape, fruit? It doesn't look anything like a grape.*

"So, this is not an orange?" I asked.

Lily and Jason laughed out loud. Jason showed me how to cut out the sections with a small knife. *I would eat it differently to avoid waste*, I voiced privately to myself. Growing up with limited resources, the habit of not wasting food, clothes, water, supplies, etc., had been engraved into my DNA. After that first grapefruit experience, I've always eaten grapefruits by peeling the outer skin off, then separating and peeling off the soft skin of each piece. It's a lot of work, but not wasting any part makes grapefruits taste much more pleasant and satisfying.

Just before we departed for school, Professor Parry returned from the guest room, holding a wet towel.

"The guest bathroom was flooded. Glad I checked it before it got worse. You did not mention any trouble you might have had," he said emotionlessly.

"Oh. Sorry. I thought I had cleaned it up already. I did not get the shower curtain in place properly." I felt my face burning. The truth was that I was initially confused about the curtain's purpose. I thought I was alone in the bathroom and thus had no privacy issues, unlike the public baths in China. Only halfway through the shower, I notice the water splashing on the floor. Even though I tried my best, my towel could not dry the floor completely. *The moisture would evaporate,* I assumed. I didn't see the need to report my ignorance.

"By the way, a friend of mine is coming for the holiday season and plans to stay with us for a few days," Jason said, subtly reminding me that I needed to find my own place soon.

I had been working on it. When I was still in China, Xiaomeng—a doctoral student in the Chemistry department who had come to the U.S. a year and a half before—had emailed me saying she'd like to share a 2-bedroom apartment with me starting January 15th.

"I got a mattress for you already. Someone threw one out yesterday," Xiaomeng emailed.

What is a mattress? I checked my dictionary immediately. Growing up in my hometown, the whole family would share one large bed made with bricks, padded with cotton beddings, and heated from underneath through built-in pathways for warmth in the winter. When I was at Peking University, we slept on bunk beds with metal frames and a thick layer of bedding on the hardwood bedboard. Mattresses sounded much more comfortable. I was grateful that Xiaomeng was handling such matters on my behalf.

January 15th was almost one month away. I needed a place for the next 28 days. I approached the student housing office on campus. The lady at the desk was busy with the computer and the phone. Once she heard me saying "room" and "apartment," she pointed me toward a plastic folder on the wall. With the help of my portable English dictionary, I finished the leasing application. Scanning the form, the lady asked a string of questions. This moment was when I realized my English was so bad. I stared at her fast-moving mouth, heard a few words I could recognize and couldn't, and had no idea what she was talking about.

"I beg your pardon...."

"Is an apartment the same as a room? I just need a room."

"Sorry, what did you say?"

"Could you repeat that one more time?"

"Did you mean, hmm...."

"Can you speak slowly..."

After about five minutes of struggling and seeing her patience fading, I pulled a pen and wrote two sentences on paper. She wrote back: "We only lease rooms by semesters starting January 15th."

To say that I felt defeated would have been an understatement. Nevertheless, I reported what happened to Professor Parry, Jason, and Lily that evening.

"Maybe you could find places in the newspaper," Lily suggested.

"Here's today's paper." Jason passed me a stack of papers.

The next day, I arrived at my office with high hopes. Using the phone on my desk, I started calling around to inquire about the places I'd circled in the newspaper.

"What do you mean unfurnished?" I asked the person on the other end of the phone. I regretted that I hadn't found out from Xiaomeng about that concept when she'd emailed me that our apartment would be unfurnished.

"Two miles from campus? Is that walkable?" *How many kilometers are two miles?* I had no sense of the distance and needed to find out later.

"Deposit? How much? Do you need it at the lease signing?" I had no money to pay for that now. Xiaomeng was so kind to have taken care of that part for me, for our apartment.

Sitting in my armchair and looking out the window onto the sunny campus, I suddenly felt the sky pressing down on me. Trying to catch tighter and tighter breaths, I reminded myself that, at least, I had a place to stay that night.

That evening, Xiaomeng invited me to a Chinese students' party in the building where my new apartment would be. Most Chinese students lived in the same building. A few lived elsewhere, including Qin and her husband, who went by the English name Mike. This was the first time I met other Chinese people.

"Hi, I'm Mr. Ma. Glad to finally meet you after hearing so much about you. Where are you staying now?" a young man asked.

"Hi, Mr. Ma, thanks. I'm staying in Professor Parry's guest room."

"You're fortunate. I've never been there but heard great things about Professor Parry's house. How long will you stay?" asked Jialing, a female doctoral student in the Philosophy department.

"Not long. I need to find a place as soon as possible—he has visitors coming."

"I would let you stay in my living room, but I've got visitors during the holidays, too," Xiaomeng said.

"We'd do the same, except our living room has no space for a mattress," Qin said, and Mike nodded.

"How about you stay in my room until I return from California? I'm leaving tomorrow," Jialing said.

"Oh? When are you back?" I asked.

"January 15th. That's the day you move into your new apartment, right? So works out perfectly," Jialing said.

"Really? Are you sure it won't be a problem for you?" I couldn't believe my luck.

"My room would be empty anyways when I'm gone. You can move in tomorrow. Just pay me one month's rent. Oh, and you can pay me once I get back. You must be tight on money right now," Jialing added.

Wow! My heart was jumping out of my chest. This would be a perfect solution.

There was also something new to me. In the old days, most of my friends and I would just let a person use an empty room for free. It was shameful to ask for compensation. Here, Jialing treated it as a matter of fact that she'd want the rent to be reimbursed. I eventually learned that both Xiaomeng and Jialing were from Shanghai. A few times in the future, they would demonstrate that they were astute businesswomen who could arrange situations that would offer mutual benefit to themselves and others. Whether Shanghainese or American savvy, I eventually liked this straightforward way of treating matters. It was hard for me to learn initially, but it proved beneficial in the long run.

I moved out of Professor Parry's place the next day. That evening, I closed Jialing's bedroom door, put my bedding on her bed, and exhaled deeply. Phew—my first challenge in the U.S. had been resolved.

Fast forward to January 15th—I moved into my apartment at 1555 Monte Vista Avenue with my roommate Xiaomeng.

She took the larger bedroom, saying, "My husband will come soon, but you're just by yourself. According to the norm, I'll pay three-fifths and you pay two-fifths when he joins me."

I was perfectly okay with that arrangement—I felt more gratitude than I could express. I now had my own bedroom and a place to cook and shower. It was much better than my living conditions in China, where four women, all junior faculty members, had shared a room about 18'x15', just enough for three bunk beds (two of the upper beds were for storing our belongings), four desks, and two bookshelves. Washrooms (for brushing teeth, washing face, and doing laundry manually) and toilets were down the hallway. We had to use public bath facilities in another building to shower or bathe.

A month later, Xiaomeng took in another Chinese student as our roommate.

"He'll use the living room—I got a curtain from a garage sale so that he can have some privacy," Xiaomeng said.

Again, I was okay with that. I hardly spent any time in the living room anyways. Arriving this late into the semester, this young man would have otherwise had a hard time finding an affordable place.

APPLE AN

Fig. 2.1 NMSU campus. 1990.

3
Friends from the Past

The morning after moving into Jialing's room, I walked to the supermarket alone. The beige-colored building had a grand entry with "Safeway" engraved in red on the top. There was an air of quietness, neatness, and cleanness compared to some big markets in Beijing where, during business hours, they'd be crowded with people hurrying through the doors or rushing out carrying big bags. The doors would never even have a chance to close. One would be lucky to find a spot to park a bike in front of the market buildings. But here, only a few people were going in or out of the entrance, which shut and opened automatically. The entire parking lot had just three or four cars.

Inside the Safeway were aisles and shelves with products I could pick up. What a big contrast to how we shopped in China, where items stayed behind counters so shoppers could not touch them. An employee or salesperson would pick up a shopper's request, collect money, then hand the products over. We usually only had a few options, and we'd often learn about a new product from friends or families before buying it.

The shopping carts and baskets here were new to me as well. I was initially puzzled by the size of the shopping carts—then I saw a couple of customers pushing their overflowing carts around. *How can people buy so many things? Maybe they have big families?*

Growing up in the 70s, we'd use our bags to carry only those products we needed immediately. By the late 80s, my habit stayed the same, even though there was no longer a government restriction on essential living resources and no shortage of food, clothing, or other products. Beijing and many other big cities had supermarkets usually owned by the government. Like Safeway, they'd carry everyday products. There were also smaller grocery stores and specialty shops, some of which were owned by individuals. From these smaller shops, one could get fresh eggs, produce from local farms, or cooked meals from local chefs. Visiting restaurants was out of the question for poor college students and professors who mainly ate in campus cafeterias with massively produced meals. Still, these smaller shops were the sources of occasional special treats.

  I spent a good hour walking around Safeway holding a basket. It was exciting, enjoyable, confusing, and overwhelming. I could see the pictures of a product or use my dictionary to find out what it was for. But I could not understand the differences among seemingly similar products. I wanted to get some drinks and remembered seeing a giant Coca-Cola bottle on the kitchen counter that morning. *That must be what everyone drinks. But what is the difference between a Coke and a Diet Coke? Oh well, just get one of each.*

When I returned, Jialing's roommate Kang shouted, "Wow, two big bottles of Coke for just one person?"

"I have friends coming tonight!" I could not hide my excitement.

"Your friends from where?" Kang's wife asked. They were having lunch in the kitchen.

"My academic brother TS, his wife, and their two friends from Louisiana. They will stop here on their way to Las Vegas for the winter break."

"I-10 is right through here; very convenient," Kang said.

"Yet, you haven't taken me anywhere," Kang's wife murmured.

"You just got here. Plus, we need to save money," Kang replied after swallowing a mouthful of food.

Back at PKU, TS had been two years ahead of me and we had the same advisor for our master's program, which made him my academic big brother. TS became a faculty member after his graduate study. We'd spent almost two years on a project. In the final year of my graduate study at PKU, I broke my ankle during ice skating and thus could not go home for the Spring Festival break. TS and his wife brought me a small black-and-white TV set, a luxury for many of us then. We later became colleagues in the same department after I joined the faculty. Last fall, at Beijing airport, I had watched him disappear through the International Departure gate to join his wife at Louisiana

State University. Before departing Beijing for America, I had emailed TS to ask if there was anything I could bring to the U.S. for him or his wife.

"Get enough pairs of glasses for yourself. They are super expensive here. Could you also bring four pairs for my wife? I'll send you the prescription," TS responded.

"What about you?" I emailed back.

"If it's not too much trouble, could you bring a good-quality set of Go? Unfortunately, it's hard to find one here." TS was a high-level player of Go, a Chinese abstract strategy board game for two players. High-quality Go sets use genuine stones rather than plastic or other materials.

When we met, he handed me a check with U.S. dollars worth more than I'd paid in Chinese Yuan and said,

"Really appreciate that you sacrificed luggage weight capacity to bring the Go for me."

"I am happy to help." I meant it. I'd gladly take any opportunity to repay anyone's kindness to me in the past.

"The biggest challenge for me initially was that I was always short of money. This must be true for you as well. I don't have much in the bank now, but this extra $400 may help you a little." He handed me another check.

"I can't take your money!"

"Relax. Think of it as a loan from me. You can pay me back when you are able." He gave me that big-brotherly expression and patted my back.

TS was right. I also found myself needing help with money. The $40 I had on me and the two checks from TS were all I had at the time. Within the first month, I bounced two checks, costing me an extra $60. I had never used anything but cash. Using checks put me in the dark. I learned a hard lesson about balancing a checkbook, especially when I had little money in the bank.

Seeing TS and his wife made me feel like I had a family in the U.S. They were two of my three close friends from PKU who were in the U.S. then. The third one was Yiqing, who had come one semester earlier to study in Minnesota. Yiqing had lived two floors above my dorm room at PKU. She and I shared a lot of interests and opinions. We had spent many days and nights at Tiananmen Square last May, just like many other PKU people did. She had already been accepted and prepared to start her doctoral study in the fall. We lost track of each other during the entire months of June and July after the Tiananmen crackdown.

"I'm safe. I'll avoid Beijing and leave my hometown in Jiangxi for the U.S. I hope to see you soon on the other side of the globe. Keep me posted on your progress," she emailed me in August before departing China.

By October, when I was finally getting everything in place to go to the U.S. except the fund for the airline ticket, I emailed her,

"I've exhausted all possible sources for the money to buy the ticket." The airfare would cost more than ten times my regular salary. I had underestimated the overall cost of preparing for the journey.

She replied immediately, "I will buy it here and ship it to you in Beijing."

That airline ticket was the last pull to get me to America.

I felt deeply in debt to my friends financially and for their affection and kindness.

Fig. 3.1 At Peking University, 1989

4
My Name is Apple

"Good morning, class!" Professor Geraldine's warm, confident voice matched the sunshine that beamed through the classroom windows.

"Good morning..."

A few quiet voices, including mine, responded, trailing off in stark contrast to hers.

I was stunned by what I saw—a beautiful middle-aged woman with short blonde hair and blue eyes. She was tall, fit, and wore a long flowy yellow dress with gray high heels. Altogether, she cut a magnificent figure.

"Welcome to Conversational English. For many of you, this class is mandatory because you need to teach in English, so let's make the best of it." She radiated, looking left and right, making eye contact with everyone.

The class mainly had Chinese students—eight or ten—and a few students from other countries. They were from all different academic majors. As I later learned, Professor Geraldine was the wife of the head of a research center affiliated with the Computer Science department. She was firm about some things, including not speaking Chinese in class. If you accidentally said a Chinese word to your classmates, you would immediately regret it under her stare.

"When I call your name, come to the front of the class and say a few words—share whatever you'd like so that your fellow classmates can get to know you," Professor Geraldine continued.

As students went up to the front and presented themselves, Professor Geraldine encouraged each of them with smiles and eye contact and said a few things in a manner that was more constructive than critical:

"I can't hear you from back here—project your voice to reach me."

"What was that again? Can you repeat what you just said slowly?"

"Look at your audience, not the ceiling when you speak."

"Reach everyone with your eyes, not just the people sitting in the front row."

"Can you spell your name out on the blackboard?"

The last question was mainly for those Chinese students whose original names were hard for some to make out just by listening. Some Chinese students had picked popular English first names. Some officially changed their first names, making their original Chinese first name into a middle name.

I decided to keep my original name, at least in some fashion. Besides the fact that it was recognizable and easy to pronounce, I valued its uniqueness. Unlike many Chinese people, whose first names had been assigned by their parents or grandparents, I had chosen my own first name or part of it. My mom gave me the sound of my name and used the most popular written character. It means flat or peace. That character was usually what people would automatically associate with when they heard the sound. But I disliked the predictability of the sound. So I selected a different character and used it in all my official documents whenever I could. I had been secretly satisfied whenever I saw people's faces reflect their surprise or appreciation when they saw the written character.

When it was my turn to go to the front, I wrote down a Chinese character on the blackboard. Immediately I heard murmurs behind me. Some Chinese students sounded it out. I then wrote the word

"Apple" next to the Chinese character and turned around to face the class.

"Hi. My name is Apple." I waved my right hand as if waving a racket. I wasn't nervous at all about speaking in front of the class, thanks to my teaching experience. By habit, my voice was naturally loud.

"Is your name really Apple?" Professor Geraldine asked.

"That is the English name I'd like to go by." I continued to tell them the story of my name and why I chose this name as my preferred name.

"Very good," Professor Geraldine nodded at me with approval.

Before letting us go that day, Professor Geraldine reviewed what had happened during class.

"Which students gave you the strongest impression so you remember their names?" she asked.

Students looked around, then, to my surprise, they all stared at me.

"That's right. Apple made the strongest impression among you all. She showed a sense of humor by associating her name with a Chinese game, which activated your memory. She also told you the meaning of her name. The result is effective—you all remember her name now and maybe will forever. And I like her inviting smile and easy manner of confidently conducting herself. So if you take the opportunity, you can make a strong, positive first impression on your students."

I'd say the same about Professor Geraldine. She had made a strong, positive first impression on me as a woman with an elegant manner and, most importantly, as a confident yet warm-hearted professor facing her class for the first time. I carried what I'd learned from her to my future teaching career. I made it a habit to dress well, smile with lots of sunshine, make eye contact with everyone in the room, and provide constructive feedback from the beginning of the class.

Since then, I have made many people smile when I tell them my name. It has been like a magic wand to break the ice with strangers. People remember my name immediately and for a long time.

Most importantly, introducing my name has always made me feel good. After all, it reminds me of Professor Geraldine. *There was once a professor who said you had a sense of humor*. And that would bring light to my day.

Fig. 4.1 NMSU campus. 1990.

5
Yolanda

During the first few weeks, I spent most of my spare time with Yolanda, Dr. Davidson's girlfriend. A single mother with two daughters, she was working on a master's degree in journalism. She had big, brown eyes, a slim, tanned face, and curly, short, brunette hair. About my height, she was slightly heavier. I never asked her age, but she seemed in her early forties. She had a soft voice and spoke slowly when talking to me. Thus I needed no help understanding her.

Yolanda took me to many places: stores, banks, her office, her daughters' playmates' homes, bars, and parties. We also went running on the track, along with Dr. Davidson. She would proudly announce to everyone we encountered, "This is my Chinese friend, Apple." When I had trouble understanding others, she would repeat slowly or rephrase so I could comprehend. She was also protective of me when we were with her friends.

"Hello, Tony. I wouldn't say that to Apple if I were you," Yolanda said, although I didn't quite get what Tony was saying.

"Mary, don't be silly. There was no such thing in China. Right, Apple?" Again, I didn't understand Mary's comment.

"Patrick, speak slowly. She just got here and is getting used to speaking English."

That made Patrick repeat his words slowly.

Yolanda's older teenage daughter was not home much because she babysat most days after school. That was refreshing: watching others' kids and getting paid instead of just as a favor like my mom made me do when I was growing up. Her younger daughter was about 10 and spent after school time playing with friends.

Yolanda and I had a matching curiosity. I was eager to absorb everything I heard, saw, and sensed about my new surroundings. She was taking in everything I could offer about Chinese culture, people, foods, my upbringing, my study and work, the books I'd read, and so on.

Being my first real American friend, much of what she said and did became my gold standard. I watched her making pizza by putting all kinds of weird toppings on it. Besides the usual sausages, olives, salami, mushrooms, peppers, etc., she would put leftovers from previous days, fruits, cereals, nuts, and almost anything.

"The fun of making your own pizza is to make it yours. No rules about what to top it with," she'd cheerfully declare.

Years later, one of my favorite dishes was pizza with a tortilla topped with all kinds of stuff I personally liked: fresh and dry fruits, nuts, veggies, or scrambled eggs.

Watching her do her makeup while driving was thrilling. With her left hand on the steering wheel, her right hand would be holding mascara, liner, lipstick, or a brush, as her eyes alternated between the mirror, dashboard, and the front window.

"Don't worry. I'm an excellent driver," she'd smile at me.

In future decades, whenever I'd have to put on lipstick or brush my hair while driving, Yolanda would pop into my mind.

Some days, Yolanda was not in the cooking mood, so she, her younger daughter, and I would just have bowls of cereal for dinner, which was fun. She never ordered takeout.

I'd show my appreciation by bringing some groceries to her home occasionally. She would eagerly look over some vegetables, such as Asian eggplants or chestnuts, and ask,

"Apple, what do you do with them? How do you cook them?"

I'd show off some of my limited cooking skills.

"So delicious!" That was her response to almost everything I presented to her.

Most of the time, Yolanda would pick me up in her car and then drop me back at my place after our meetings. A few times, I had to walk from my home to hers, which would take about 20 minutes. I had no problem with such a short walk, as I had been used to walking since childhood.

"Does it take about the same time to walk to your office from your place?" She asked one day.

"Yes, about 20 minutes."

"You'll have to do the same walk every day once school starts."

"Yes, that's fine."

"Would you like to use that old bike in my backyard? It may need some work."

Bikes were the primary personal transportation tools in China. In the 60s, when I was still little, not every family had a bike. I felt thrilled and proud when a relative carried my sister and me home on his bike after picking us up from the daycare center. Many kids looked on from behind the fenced gate with envy. After my parents divorced in 1973 when I was 10, we moved to a new home. Since we had no bike, my mom had to walk 15 minutes to work each way, and we kids had to walk 20 minutes to school. Having no bike was especially difficult when we would have to shop and carry heavy items home, such as bags of rice or flour.

My mom got a new bike when I started middle school. She would carry either one or both of us to school on her way to work, depending on whether she was also taking other stuff. Those were precious moments we shared with her. During my last year of middle school, my father finally passed on an old bike to us. It was a 26-inch green bike with a downward-sloping top bar, thus named a lady's bike since ladies could get on even if they were wearing skirts. He had built the bike himself when he was taken to one of the re-education camps during the Cultural Revolution. It had always been too small for his 180 cm (5'11") frame, but he kept it so that we could not have it—one of many nasty things he did in retaliation to my mom's request for divorce. The small green bike had seen better days when it came to us. The air would escape the tires every few days because replacing the inner tubes—which had been patched countless times—would require money, and we already had a small air pump at home thus it cost nothing to fill the tires. However, it did give us the joy of riding to school. Usually, I rode, and my sister sat in the back. That bike eventually gave up entirely after a couple of years.

During my college entrance exams, my mom skipped work and waited outside the test center with her bike, so I wouldn't have to walk home after long hours of exams. For most of my college years in the early 80s, I walked everywhere on the vast campus. More and more students started to have bikes. The parking lots in front of the library, the cafeterias, and the classroom buildings were full of bikes. There were even bike shelters built along with the new student dormitories. In my senior year, my mom got me a used bike from one of her friends. It was a 28-inch lady's bike with faded, wine-red paint. The owner gave her a good deal, explaining, "I wish my kids could attend PKU. I'm honored that this bike will be ridden on the PKU campus." After my mom bought it, I still had to wait for a couple of months until a truck from her workplace delivered something to Beijing. I loved this bike, my very first one, for the color and style. Its handlebars were higher than those on either the small green bike or my mom's bike, making me feel I was sitting taller and more elegantly. It had to be fixed frequently but accompanied me for four years.

When graduate school ended and I was hired to teach, I received the only gift from my paternal grandfather: a brand-new, 26-inch lady's bike.

"This is to congratulate you on becoming a professor at Peking University," he had said, handing me the key to the lock on the bike.

Coincidently, this new bike was a shade of dark red too, reminding me of my first bike. This bike would have cost me four months' salary. Since my grandfather had gifted it to me, I just needed to spend a fraction of my salary on decorating it with a seat cover, a handlebar-mounted basket, and some wraps around the front frame so that my shoes wouldn't scratch the paint by accident. Though I cared about all my belongings, I took extra care toward this new bike. I'd park it far from any entry since there would be fewer bikes and thus less chance for it to be buried or damaged by other bikes if they fell. At night, I always parked it inside the bike shelter.

Before I left China, I gave away most of my belongings to family members and close friends. My mom wanted my bike even though she did not need another one. After I arrived in the U.S., I had multiple dreams of it being abandoned in the bike shelter. Years later, my sister told me it was still inside the bike shelter where I last parked it. My mom never had a chance to transport it back to our hometown.

Yolanda's old bike was green too, which reminded me of the small green bike my father had built, though this one looked very different—more muscular. It indeed needed attention. Every 50 yards or so, I'd have to stop to put the chain back in place. But it was still my first bike in the U.S., carrying me 50 yards at a time.

Days passed quickly. Soon, Christmas music dominated the radio in Yolanda's car.

"What's your plan for Christmas?" She asked one day.

"Don't know. You?"

"The girls will be with their dad. Would you like to come with me to visit my parents in Cloudcroft?"

"Of course! Where is Cloudcroft?"

"About one and a half hours away, towards the northeast. Have you ever celebrated Christmas?"

"No. I've heard this is the biggest holiday in the U.S.?"

"True. How about I pick you up at 9 a.m. tomorrow?"

This trip was my first time traveling outside Las Cruces. After driving through some desert, tall trees and mountains rose around us, signaling we'd just crossed into a different world. I was amazed by the quiet road—we only saw a handful of cars along the way. The car ride felt a lot shorter than I'd expected. After passing a few houses in a small village, Yolanda stopped the car in front of a stand-alone, one-story building. She carried bags to the door while I lingered briefly to take a deep breath. The air was fresh and chilly, with a strong pine smell.

"Mama and Papa, this is my friend Apple," Yolanda said.

Papa nodded at me. He was quiet and spoke only a few words during our two-day stay. Mama gave me a warm hug, which I was getting used to now. We joined them inside, where they put our bags into the guest room and invited us into the kitchen to chat.

"You're so skinny—what do you normally eat?" Mama examined me from head to toe.

I had never heard people say I was skinny, partly because I was taller and bigger than most Chinese women in my generation and partly because I had always struggled with my weight.

"Noodles, rice, vegetables, eggs, fish and shrimp, pork and chicken."

"What would you eat during your biggest holidays?" Mama asked again.

"In my hometown, we make dumplings during the Spring Festival."

"Do they look like these?" She showed me some dumplings with thick skin and neat edges, almost as if made by a machine.

"Not exactly. What kind of dumplings are these?" I was half excited and half puzzled. *They have dumplings too?*

Mama said a word I could not recognize.

"Italian dumplings. They are filled with potatoes and cheese," Yolanda said.

"What do Chinese dumplings look and taste like?" Mama asked.

I was eager to show them Chinese dumplings. Fortunately, they had white flour and ground beef. That would do.

"Do you have some rollers to make the dumpling skins?" I asked.

Mama opened a drawer and took out a roller thick in the middle with handles at both ends: "You mean like this one?"

"Oh, it's too big. Any smaller ones?" In my hometown, we used big rollers—even longer than this—to make noodles, but smaller rollers—about one foot long and a little thicker than the thumb—to make dumpling skins.

"This is the only one we have. We use it to make Mexican food."

It was not ideal, but I could make it work.

"Could I have a small pot to boil some water?" I asked after finishing up five dumplings.

"What is it for?" Mama asked while holding out a saucepan.

"I need to taste the stuffing to see if it is salty enough. Because it has raw meat, I must cook it."

"Can't you use the microwave?" Mama asked.

I had never seen a microwave before. A few minutes later, I learned that using a microwave for cooking dumplings was not a good idea—it dried the juice, burned the meat, and made the wrap hard.

"They should look and taste a lot better," I was anxious to explain.

"I trust you." Mama smiled.

Mama and Yolanda joined me in making dumplings after I told them that Chinese families, primarily women in the families, usually do so together to socialize during holidays.

I got plenty of compliments on the taste of the dumplings—even from Papa—though I thought I could have done better if I'd had all the necessary ingredients and tools.

Before bedtime, I spotted wrapped gift boxes under a beautifully decorated Christmas tree. A horrible feeling rose in me: I had not brought anyone any gifts!

"Don't worry. You are doing fine. You'll see in the morning," Yolanda said reassuringly, almost as if I was her teenage daughter.

In the morning, I found a box under the Christmas tree with my name on it. Inside was a beautiful hairpin from Yolanda.

She held a box indicating it was a gift from me to her. Then, smiling at my mystified face, she opened it before me. It was the Butterfly Lover music cassette I had given her during our second meeting eight days ago.

"Thank you for the gift. I love this music." She gave me a bear hug and I hugged her back.

The two days were filled with laughter and delicious food. My uneasiness disappeared. I joined Mama in whatever she was doing. She was eager to explain everything I might have a question about. Yolanda and I took a pleasant walk outside, where the forest was refreshing and therapeutic. Over the next few months, I'd drive my own car to visit Mama and Papa a few more times without Yolanda and re-experienced the calming force of the forest. I was humbled and honored when Mama said I was like her adopted daughter.

The end of the semester came, and the graduation ceremony was happening in May.

During my time at Peking University, there was no formal graduation ceremony, graduation gowns, hats, hoods, or a moment for family and friends to celebrate together. Instead, each class might gather to take a graduation photo that showed the Boya Pagoda in the background, a famous landmark on the PKU campus, but that was it.

At NMSU, graduation was a significant event, and I was looking forward to it for days beforehand. But, besides the fact that it was new to me, the most important reason was that Yolanda was graduating.

I accompanied her the entire morning. I watched her put on makeup carefully, fit the hat with numerous bobby pins, stretch out her gown, and test the hood. The gown was deep royal blue, the hood yellow and red—all colors I liked.

"Would you like to try them on?" Yolanda must have read what was on my mind.

"Oh my god, of course!" I was thrilled.

"We must fold the hat a bit—you've got a big head. The hat doesn't fit." Yolanda maneuvered the hat briefly and flattened it on my head. I looked into the long mirror on the door of her bedroom. Wow! I looked fancy and different in the whole package.

I look forward to the day I wear all these for my own graduation!

Yolanda and I arrived at the auditorium. She marched in and sat in the center with rows of foldable chairs. I could only sit way back in the audience section. Each student's name was read out, and they walked up on the stage to shake hands with a few people there and get a hardcover booklet. I was impatiently waiting for Yolanda's name to be read—and then it was, and her big moment was over in a blink of an eye. I had to wait for the rest of the list to be read before greeting her in person. Dr. Davidson was there, too, although he was sitting in the faculty section during the entire ceremony. Once it was over, I met both and took a few photos.

Yolanda moved to Utah after graduation. We stayed in touch by phone for a while, but then life got in the way. I hope someday we will meet again.

6
First TV Set

"Damn it! Come on!" Mr. Ma frantically pounded the TV to make the picture clearer. It was in the middle of a popular show.

"Moving the antenna this way can help. It happens many times," his wife said, jumping off the couch to help. The two put their heads together and moved the TV set and the antenna around for quite a while, but there was little improvement.

"How old is this TV?" I asked.

I was visiting Mr. Ma and his wife. Mr. Ma was a doctoral student in the Physics department. His wife had joined him a few months earlier. They lived downstairs in the same apartment building as me. I had overheard others saying that Mr. Ma was lucky to have the best TV among all the Chinese students.

"Who knows? We got it from a garage sale. I swear it was very good just yesterday," Mr. Ma said, pounding the TV set and moving the antenna again. The fuzzy, distorted images remained fuzzy and distorted.

I saw his wife rolling her eyes.

"Is that where all other Chinese got their TVs?" I asked.

At the first party I'd attended in the U.S., people talked about certain TV shows as if they had all watched them. That gave me the impression that every Chinese student had a TV.

That would be a significant improvement in the lives of these people who came to the U.S. from China. TV sets were still considered luxury items for many Chinese households then.

The first time I watched television was in the mid-1970s, in my early teen years. A 9-inch, black-and-white TV set stood on the windowsill in a community center, facing an open yard. People brought stools, chairs, and benches to the yard. More than 30 people gathered. Young children were ordered to sit on the ground up front. Grownups neatly staggered themselves so everyone could manage to see the small screen. I was awestruck. Even though we only watched images of the countryside or people working in a factory as part of a news briefing, seeing moving human beings on that tiny screen was magical.

By the late 1970s, after the Cultural Revolution, China started to open up to other countries to exchange ideas, experiences, goods, and business development. Some government workers had the opportunity to make overseas trips. As a reward for their service, these people were given a purchasing allowance of two items from a luxury goods list, including TVs, washing machines, refrigerators, watches, and stereos. No one else could buy them without those allowance tickets, even if they had enough money. Upon returning home, the workers would go to the Overseas Service Department to pick up their requested items. Some were made in China, and some were imported. The most popular watches were made in Switzerland. For refrigerators, Siemens from Germany and Toshiba from Japan were hot brands. The most desirable color TVs were made in Japan.

In the mid-1980s, government allowance and restrictions disappeared. People could buy TVs from department stores freely if they had the money. Most available TV brands were made in China. They had fluffy images and were of lower quality than the imported ones. Still, many households needed more spare money to buy luxury items. Some could only afford black-and-white or a small color TV made in China. A household's socioeconomic status was symbolized by whether it had a set and, if so, what type.

"Yes. Of course. Everyone gets TVs from garage sales," Mr. Ma said with a surprised expression as if saying, "What kind of a question was that?"

"How much did you pay for it?" My curiosity increased.

"We paid $50 and got a really good one," Mr. Ma's face lit up.

"Others would pay somewhere between $30 to $60. It is not guaranteed to be good," his wife added.

This one was not good at all.

What's the point of having a TV but constantly struggling with the signal? To people like us, whose native language was not English and who had no cultural background in the U.S., we needed every opportunity to learn, including watching TV without interruptions. A good TV seemed like a necessity. The money should be considered well spent.

When my first paycheck of $850 for being a Teaching Assistant came, I asked a friend with a car to take me to Walmart. Among the displayed units, I found a 21" RCA color TV a good choice due to its quality ratio to price. It was priced at $199 plus tax.

Since the living room of my apartment was used as a third bedroom, I had to put the new TV in my bedroom. This was a perfect setting because it allowed me to watch during every spare moment I had.

Two days after I bought the TV, Professor Parry chatted with me before class.

"I heard you got a brand-new RCA TV," Professor Parry said.

"Yes, I did. Did you hear it from Lily or Jason?"

"No, I heard it from two other Chinese students."

"Oh, interesting. I guess people talk."

"Yes, they do. But, you know, you are one unique Chinese person, very different from the others."

"Because I bought a new TV?"

"Yes, and more. You've done other things too that few Chinese have done."

Okay then. I would ask him later what he was referring to. But I did hear from others that I was different, doing things like mingling with Americans from the first moment I arrived in the U.S., going to the bank myself to open an account, and registering for courses without checking with others about how difficult the professors of those courses might be.

The 21" RCA color TV was with me for the next twenty-six years, though the remote control gave up eventually. That TV always had the sharpest image of all the sets I owned. In 2016, I gave it away for free at a neighborhood garage sale because no one in my home watched TV anymore. It was still working and still sharp.

Fig. 6.1. A brand-new RCA. 1990. Las Cruces, NM.

7
Dropped-Noodle Soup

I had left home at 17 to go to college in Beijing and had hardly ever felt homesick during the almost ten years I'd spent there. But about five weeks after coming to the U.S., I was sick. Symptoms? One was feeling lonely. I couldn't call my mom or any relatives because they were not accessible by phone. I tried twice to call my long-time professor's home in Beijing, but both failed, and I was charged $5 for each try. One just had to hate—and love—AT&T. Other symptoms? Lack of sleep at night, lack of energy during the day, lack of appetite, and lack of desire to do anything. I even had to excuse myself from attending classes one day.

Word passed around that I was not well. First came my roommate Xiaomeng, then the neighbors, all asking if anything could be done to make me feel better.

"I want my mom's dropped-noodle soup," I murmured to Xiaomeng.

Being Shanghainese, she had never had that kind of soup before. It was a northern Chinese homemade meal I'd had since a very early age.

"Good news. I've been asking around and finally found out Ralph knows how to make it," Xiaomeng said as if she'd found the medicine for a severe disease.

Until then, I might have only said "Hi" twice and hardly paid attention to this Ralph guy who lived just a few doors from me in the same building. It might be because he was not an in-your-face person—he was slightly shorter than me, had a thin frame, a pair of oversized glasses, and a small, thin mustache. However, I did see him sitting in Professor Parry's undergraduate classes where I was a TA. I'd also noticed that he owned a bike with a flat tire and a car that occasionally spewed black smoke from the back as it went along. Few other Chinese students had cars, and only a couple had bikes, so these items made him a rich guy.

"Ralph came from Stanford University. He adopted that name because his Chinese name is impossible to pronounce by Americans. His wife is the most beautiful lady I have ever seen. She is a nurse in California and makes a lot of money," Xiaomeng continued.

That evening, Ralph brought a bowl of dropped-noodle soup. It was not even close to what my mom made. He told me that he had researched how to cook one. *Okay, the thought and the effort count.* Not being used to such kind treatment, I was touched.

Ralph became a frequent visitor for the next couple of days. After I told him how my mom made the soup, he produced it almost as good as my mom's. He had good reasons to knock on the door of our apartment.

"Be careful. He has a wife," Xiaomeng warned me one day. She did not hide her opinion of him.

"Yes, I know. He told me he is in the process of getting a divorce."

"I can see why. Do you know he grew up in the country?" Xiaomeng was among those who were serious about one's social class.

During the Cultural Revolution from 1966-1976, farmers from the countryside or blue-collar workers in the cities were favored and ranked highest in classes because they were considered purer, with fewer anti-party thoughts or actions. Meanwhile, educated, white-collar workers who mostly lived in cities were regarded toward the bottom of the social hierarchy and were the targets of Red Guards' attacks. That designation was reversed entirely after the Cultural Revolution ended in 1976. People in big cities, especially those from families with some education, considered themselves superior to blue-collar workers or anyone from the countryside.

"They grew up with different values than people like us who grew up in big cities." She had a point. But at that time, I didn't think the conversation was relevant.

Several other single Chinese guys started to show me their attention. One of them was from my English class. Originally from Tianjin, he was tall, fit, good looking, and his glasses made him look like a sensible scholar. The problem was that I found his IQ was lower than his looks. Plus, he was shy and laid-back, which made him a loser in any competition.

The second guy was a graduate student in my department. He was from Taiwan, spoke fluent English, had a proud sense of being from a royal family, and had a fancy car he'd promise to let people—including me—drive. He bragged a lot, which quickly lost my respect. He was not afraid to show attention to me in front of a large group. He'd try to stop by whenever he saw my office door open, which was quite often because I had to hold office hours. Standing by the door, he'd talk non-stop about many things at a superficial level. Sometimes, I had to close the door when I saw him around the hallway's corner. Whenever possible, I avoided him.

The third guy was from another department who had come to the university a few semesters earlier. He had the looks and the IQ and had the experience of living in the U.S. longer than most of us. I found him a good conversationalist during our limited interactions. He hosted a party at his apartment to celebrate Chinese New Year. I accepted his invitation and found that the Tianjin guy was at the party too. All the other guests were non-Chinese. As the party went on, the Tianjin guy and I realized that we were there to make dumplings for the party. *He only sees people as some kind of useful tool.*

Ralph frequently visited not only my apartment but also my office. He had a legitimate reason: "Some course materials were hard to understand." Most of my office hours were occupied by him, and he had no sympathy for any students who needed my help. I complained once to him but eventually let it be. Besides course-related questions, we also randomly chatted about this or that. It was easy and fun to talk with him.

Gradually, I found myself wishing he'd drop by.

When he asked me out for our first date, I said yes. It was dinner at a steakhouse. Ralph had promised that it would be the best meal I had ever had. As it turned out, I only remembered the square-shaped A1 bottle because it was passed between us frequently. I could not recall the actual taste of the steak, and I was not impressed. Either the steak could have been better, or I was not a red-meat fan.

One evening, I had to work late in my office. Under the pressure of Ralph's persistent requests, I visited his office for the first time. Unlike mine, which had two big windows, his office had no windows in the middle of the building. Like my officemate, who was rarely there, his officemate was missing most of the time too. Closing the office door, he pulled me into his arms and kissed me. I closed my eyes, feeling a burning and breathless sensation in my brain, mouth, heart, and whole body. My feet were literally off the ground. My head was in the clouds as he pulled me to his lap. That was my first kiss ever.

Whereas I had hardly noticed him initially, he told me he'd seen me the second day after I'd moved to Jialing's room. I was on my way to Safeway.

"You were wearing a yellow PKU sweatshirt with a high ponytail. You looked beautiful, healthy, full of energy, and confident. I was intrigued," he recalled.

That same evening, he saw me again when my academic brother TS and his friends visited.

"Your hair was down, and you were smiling sweetly. That was when I fell in love with you."

I vaguely remembered a group of guys playing cards in the kitchen then. He must have been one of them.

We progressed steadily in our relationship, albeit under the radar. Ralph had received the final divorce papers. I never really figured out why his marriage had not worked, and he did not want to elaborate on the details. Other Chinese people told me that his wife, working as a nurse now in California, was a doctor by training who had grown up in Beijing. She had highly educated parents, a family with good connections and backgrounds, and an army of young men pursuing her. She was 173 cm (5'8") tall, at least 9 cm (3") taller than him. I only saw one picture in which the two stood side by side, with him struggling to put his right arm around her shoulders. In that photo, he was beaming widely, but there was an air of sadness on her face. She had a naturally downcast face with her eyebrows falling on the sides. According to Chinese face readings, this indicated a hard life ahead of her.

They were married in Beijing. A few months later, he went to Stanford to continue his graduate study. She quit her job as a doctor and joined him as a spouse. But before long, he decided to change his major from geology to computer science. He enrolled in the Ph.D. program at NMSU one semester before I arrived. He had to take a few undergraduate computer science courses to compensate for his lack of training in the field. His wife had visited him briefly in Las Cruces but then returned to California and found a job. The Christmas break after I arrived, he'd driven his little car to California to see if there was any hope for his marriage. What he got was his wife's plea: "Please let me go."

Ralph would often sneak into my room without alarming my two roommates. Sometimes I'd go to his apartment to cook meals and do my homework since Ralph's roommate worked hard and was rarely home. One time in his apartment, he showed me a hole in his backpack, and I was eager to show off my sewing skills. I was also happy to sing my favorite song, the Carpenters' "Yesterday Once More," to him.

This was also when I developed mysterious red rashes all over my body, which always came at night but would disappear during the day. Incredibly itchy, hot, and uncomfortable, my sleeping was jeopardized, further affecting my daily activities. Finally, after it had happened a few times, Ralph suggested I go to the emergency room, my first visit to such a place in the U.S. We arrived very early. I had the symptoms on my body when I was checked in. But when I was called in four hours later, I was a healthy person with nothing to show to the doctor.

The recommendation to "take some Benadryl if it happens again" was the only outcome of the visit. The four-hour-long wait was so irritating that I made a mental note to avoid the ER as much as possible.

During those uncomfortable days, Ralph was tender and caring. Never been attended to by a man, I was truly touched.

Two months after I'd arrived in the U.S., on Valentine's Day, Ralph asked me to be his girlfriend. He became my first boyfriend in every sense. The rashes disappeared as mysteriously as they'd arrived.

8
THE WHEELS

Ralph's 1973 Nissan was a tiny manual transmission car that could seat five people—if they were all skinny. He took three other people and me to shop for Asian food in El Paso. One guy sat on the passenger seat beside him and three ladies were in the back. I was sitting on the left side, and the lady in the middle was almost sitting on top of me. We made a "wow" sound and readjusted with every car turn.

Until then, I had never touched the steering wheel of a car.

One day I asked Ralph, "Can you teach me how to drive?"

"Of course! But you must first study the rules and signs and pass the written test," he said. He took me to the Department of Motor Vehicles to request a driver's handbook. Besides some factual data that I had to remember, such as legal alcohol levels, most rules and signs made sense. Two days later, I passed the test and received my learning permit. Ralph drove me to an empty parking lot.

"You need to learn how to park first. Then drive backward, and lastly forward." His voice was full of authority.

"Now, put your hands at the 10 and 2 o'clock positions. This will allow you to steer the car easily and quickly without too many hand movements."

I put my hands there and looked at the dashboard.

"Look at the front, not the dashboard," he responded immediately.

I looked up. That reminded me that I'd been told something similar by a friend—to look up instead of down—when I was learning how to ride a bike.

"Your right foot is the most important: it controls the brake and the gas pedal. Don't ever mix those two up."

I blinked. *Okay, noted.*

"Now, your left foot will determine if the car is alive or dead, go or stop."

Huh?

"It controls the clutch, which allows you to shift among gears. A gear is either going backward or forward at different speeds," he continued.

"Where is the gear?" I asked.

"On your right-hand side. You shift with your right hand."

"But you said I should put my right hand in the 2 o'clock position."

"Whenever you don't need to shift the gears, you need to hold the steering wheel."

"So, my left hand must be strong enough to control the wheel alone?"

"Correct. All four limbs must work together in a coordinated way."

I blinked again. *Sounds complicated.* I used my left hand to turn the wheel, but it would not move.

"It's too heavy for one hand," I said.

"It won't be once the engine is on," Ralph answered.

"The engine is not on?" I looked at the dashboard.

"Did you turn it on?" He laughed.

For the next several minutes, I turned on the engine, and it died; I turned it on again, and again it died.

"Keep your left foot on the clutch until your gear is in the right place, and you'll be ready to go."

I turned on the engine again, and this time it kept running. I changed the gear and let go of the left foot, and the car died.

"Lift the left foot gradually and, at the same time, slowly use the right foot to push for gas. The two feet need to coordinate."

I exhaled a long breath. The engine was on, the gear was in the first position, the left and right feet coordinated, and the car went backward. A panic hit me, and I braked. The car died.

"Good progress. Keep going." Ralph seemed to be enjoying the moment.

Over the next hour, I made the car stop, jump, die, restart, make squeaking sounds, and shake violently at times. We often lurched toward the front window and threw our heads back into the headrests. Yet, marvelously, the car moved forward or backward several yards at a time. And I could make this happen repeatedly.

"Let's go to campus," Ralph said calmly.

"What if I hit somebody or some car?"

"As long as you stay in your lane and use the brake when necessary, you'll be fine."

The next moment, I was driving on local roads. Even though the car died almost every time a traffic light turned from red to green, I only received one honk. Almost everyone waited patiently for me to restart the vehicle.

Soon I was driving around the city, which took little time since it was so small. I made progress at the traffic lights such that the car died only about a third of the time when the lights changed. My plea, "Stay green, stay green, please!" might have also worked whenever I approached a traffic light.

"Let's go to El Paso," Ralph said as if suggesting we go for dinner.

"What? That means we must get on I-10."

"Exactly."

"But what if the car dies on the highway?"

"It won't. It may die on local roads, which is fine."

"But, but. I have only been learning to drive for two hours."

"So what? You're ready. Just remember, don't hesitate. Once you decide to enter a lane or make a turn, just stay with it. I'll help you figure out when to change lanes."

I thought about the idea for a few seconds. *Yeah, so what? The car has died so many times, and nothing terrible has happened. I can handle the car if it's moving. Okay, let's go with it.*

I did not realize that when there were so many cars driving next to me so closely at such a high speed, it felt a lot more intimidating, and my hands started to shake.

"You are doing fine. Push for gas. That is the only way to keep the car going."

Geez, where does his confidence in me come from? I could kill both of us.

The thrill of driving on the highway for 45 minutes was so intense that my heart was in my throat the entire time. The satisfaction and pride I felt after we arrived at the Asian store in El Paso were so high that I wanted to drive again and again. *I got the wheels*!

9
Driving to the West

Several people, including the Tianjin and Taiwanese guys, asked me about my spring break plans long before spring break. Almost every Chinese student looked forward to sharing cars to go to faraway places for those nine days. But, of course, Ralph had been planning on it, too, a trip for just the two of us. Since his car was unreliable, Ralph went to pick up a rental car on the day we were to depart. He came back with a disturbed expression on his face.

"I just became the common enemy of all local Chinese," Ralph snarled.

As it turned out, he had a confrontation with several single Chinese guys when fighting for the last rental car. It didn't help once they learned I'd turned down their invitations because I was going away with Ralph. Many Chinese, including my roommate Xiaomeng, were shocked and somehow outraged about our relationship. He was seen as an experienced, married man, out to trick and trap me, an innocent girl. People were still friendly to me, but few would talk to him after this rental car incident.

Our trip was to drive west. Ralph got a booklet of maps from AAA that outlined our journey. With few cars and no traffic, I handled the rental car easily during the first few hours on westbound I-10. Besides seeing the scenery and experiencing whatever would come our way, driving remained my most significant interest. On the other hand, Ralph would happily sleep in the passenger seat as much as possible.

For our first break, we stopped at a service station with no other customers. This was the first time I'd used a service station. It had restrooms and picnic tables in the shade. We sat at a table to have salads and sandwiches I'd packed the night before. Back in China, packing snacks and meals had always been something I enjoyed. In middle and high school, we would have field trips to help farms in the countryside or do physical labor at a factory. My mom usually made hard-boiled eggs with tea leaves and soy sauce, spread preserved tofu jam inside a bun, and packed everything in a tin box. Occasionally, I might find a piece of candy, a tomato, or a cucumber in the box. In college, there were a few outings organized by the students. We usually had to pack our food because few places we'd visit would have markets. So packing food for trips became something more than just preparing meals. There was the expectation, imagination, and anticipation of what or where we might eat and with whom. On all these occasions, we had no ice bags or coolers. We just hoped that our packed meals would still be fresh by the time we ate them.

For this spring break trip, we bought a cooler that was so spacious we could pack a salad, salad dressing, bread, peanut butter, jelly, milk, soda, snack bars, and chocolate candies. But one thing remained the same: food tasted much better when consumed outside the house with traveling companions.

We continued along the highway. Both sides were deserts with low bushes, a little color, and nothing interesting. But things started to change once we got closer to Arizona. The bushes got higher and greener, and one after the other, cactus trees appeared, all of them shooting toward the sky. I'd never seen such trees.

"Let's stop here." I parked the car on the roadside.

"You'll see a lot of them," Ralph said.

"But I want to see this one," I exclaimed, running up the hill. Finally, I stopped in front of a tall cactus tree.

APPLE AN

It stood there by itself with an air of pride. Its trunk was thick, its height many times mine. I touched the scars on the stem. It must have been the wind and sun that had left various shades of brown colors and roughened the surface. I looked up—its branches were young-looking, green, vigorous, and strong. They were like siblings at different ages, each trying to outrace the others to be the first to reach the sky. I walked around the tree with increased admiration. Straight-spined, healthy, and full of life, it humbled me; I felt small and insignificant.

Fig. 9.1 Somewhere in Arizona, March 1990

We continued through Arizona. Tucson seemed like a bald guy to me, and Phoenix was like a lady in a pretty dress or a lady getting dressed because there was so much construction going on. I faced my first driving challenge in Phoenix. Ongoing construction had left two lanes very narrow. I got stuck on the inside lane bordered by blocks that protected the road from oncoming cars. My car's right mirror almost touched other vehicles in the outside lane. So many times, I worried that I would hit either the blocks or the other cars. My mind was vigilant, and my arms were tight as if holding a heavy weight. I had to keep driving because there was no way to stop or get out of there. It would have been nice if I had gotten some supervision or emotional support from Ralph. But the entire time, he slept soundly, without worrying about my driving or psychological state.

From Phoenix, we drove to Las Vegas, a city Ralph had told me about several times. I got the impression that Las Vegas represented the U.S. in a significant way. Seeing the city emerge from a deserted horizon was jaw-dropping. Once in the city, I found the buildings magnificent, the signs and lights dazzling. This was the fanciest and most glorious city I had ever seen.

We checked into a hotel and entered a windowless room with basic furniture and facilities.

I was unimpressed: "I stayed in better hotel rooms while traveling in China."

"People don't spend time in their room except to sleep. But we can eat all we want without paying much. They want us to gamble so that they can make money," said Ralph.

We went immediately to the buffet. The dining hall was humongous, with many sitting areas and choices for food. We had been looking forward to this meal and had prepared by starving ourselves for the past several hours. I sampled as much as possible and stuffed myself so full that I just wanted to sit there and rest.

"Come on. Let's go and play." Ralph was eager to show me more.

The game floor was dark and crowded. The cigarette smoke made my eyes and throat hurt. We walked around to check out various types of games. I did not know how to play any of those games. The only ones I could play were slot machines. They ate quarters like I was cracking shelled sunflower seeds, except nothing was spat out. Ah, wait a moment! Just as my quarters were used up, a bunch of quarters came out to hit the drawer-shaped container like hail hitting the ground. I won a basketful of quarters.

"Should we keep them and go now?" I was so excited. I had never won anything before, and these seemed like quite a lot of money to a poor student.

"Let's play them all," Ralph suggested. I learned later that he believed one could either get money or love, but not both. Before we left for the trip, we had set up rules for Vegas: not losing more than $20. We stopped playing when we reached that limit. By then, I was eager to leave the dark and smoky hall. I found more joy in driving around the many captivating scenes in Vegas and taking pictures.

Next, I wanted to see the ocean for the first time. We got on the Pacific Coast Highway or Route 1 northward from Santa Monica. Then, we changed to Route 101 toward Santa Barbara, with the ocean on my left the whole time. I rolled down the window and drove as slowly as traffic allowed. The air filled with a slightly salty, slightly wet odor. The calm wind gently brushed my face and ears as the early morning sun shone on the water, creating waves of sparkles. The vast and endless horizon blended so it was hard to tell where the water met the sky.

For the first time, I felt possessed by the endlessness and limitlessness of time and space. No worries, no burdens, no thoughts, and no emotions. The deliciousness of my disappearing from my own consciousness was way beyond what I had expected from Ralph's description of the ocean before the trip.

We stopped in a quiet, undeveloped spot so I could touch the water. The close contact with the ocean drastically differed from admiring it in the distance. The brown beach had small rocks, shells, and dead seaweed. I could hear only the waves, nothing else. I removed my shoes and socks and put my feet in the chilly water. It sent shocks through my whole body and soul that lasted a few seconds. Then my feet became numb to the temperature, yet still sensitive to the water's softness. I fixed my eyes on one wave at a time as it collapsed at my feet. I could not help but play with the waves that rushed toward me by chasing and retreating. At that moment, nothing else mattered, time stopped, and the rest of the world disappeared.

I did not know how long it had been when Ralph finally took my arm and gestured that we needed to move on. We reached a marina right outside Santa Barbara. Sailboat after sailboat, some docked, some on the way out, and many already on the water. Seagulls flew above us, making playful sounds. Children shouted and laughed on a nearby beach.

Fig. 9.2 Pacific Ocean, March 1990

Sitting on a bench and taking in all my surroundings, I suddenly realized that China was just on the other side of the ocean. It felt so close, yet so far away. It was only three months ago that I had been in Beijing, yet I felt like that was an ancient time. I was amazed at how far I had come physically, emotionally, and spiritually. There was so much I had let go and left behind; so much more was unknown, challenging, and exciting to look forward to. I pinched my leg to bring myself back to reality. *I am here, for real, sensing such vital freedom and unlimited potential that I should treasure and use wisely.*

Our next stop was Los Angeles. I wanted to visit my friends Fanfan and Young, who lived outside UCLA. Both were from PKU, Fanfan had been my roommate in graduate school and Young was a mutual friend. The summer before, I was surprised when Young took a break from studying at UCLA and flew to Beijing to get a marriage certificate with Fanfan. They invited several other friends and me for a celebration at a restaurant in Beijing. Soon after that, Fanfan left Beijing to join Young in Los Angeles.

"This is my friend Ralph, also from my university. We're traveling together for spring break." I introduced Ralph to Fanfan and Young.

"Welcome. We only have one pullout sofa. Is it okay for you to sleep on the living room floor tonight?" Fanfan did not suspect we were dating.

"Yes, that's fine." Ralph gave me a nod.

"So glad to see you. Remember Dawei, the guy I told you about in the email?" Fanfan turned to me and continued, "He's coming for dinner."

Oh no. I had completely forgotten about this guy that Fanfan had told me about almost two months ago. She wanted to match us up as a couple. Single Chinese males had tremendous trouble finding a spouse in the U.S.

Young prepared the dinner, and Dawei brought two bottles of wine. As it turned out, Dawei was as handsome as Fanfan had described in the email. Our brief conversations indicated he had a bright mind as well. He was attentive and charming after an initial shyness. *He is a nice guy with potential. But it's too late... I have Ralph now.* The following day, before Fanfan and Young got up, Ralph pulled me into his arms and kissed me hard.

I was so glad that Fanfan and Young seemed in love. Fanfan was not the ice queen anymore, and Young seemed caring and attentive. I was especially moved when Young told a story of when he went to Fanfan's restaurant to wash dishes on her behalf because she claimed she had a woman's special day that gave her cramps.

Years later, Young found a teaching job in Hong Kong after getting his Ph.D. because, at that time for his area of study, the ratio for a faculty position to the number of graduates was 1 to 200 in the U.S. I last met him in Hong Kong in 1999 when I had a visiting professorship at a Hong Kong university. I brought their boy a set of cars.

"Did my mom ask you to give the cars to me?" The seven-year-old had asked, his big eyes wide open. He reminded me so much of his mom.

I did not know what to say. I did not want to lie, but I did not want to hurt that innocent heart either.

"Do you miss your mom?" I asked instead.

"Yes. She calls. But I want to see her."

Fanfan hated Hong Kong and grew depressed. My fears were confirmed—they divorced shortly after moving to Hong Kong. I sometimes wondered if Young had never gotten over another girl who had lived in our dorm. I thought he married Fanfan for three reasons: he was lonely in the U.S., the other girl was in a relationship already, and Fanfan had proposed to him. I never figured out why Fanfan did it, given she was regarded as the most beautiful girl on the PKU campus and had a long line of young suitors both within and outside PKU. After the divorce, Fanfan returned to the U.S., leaving the boy with Young in Hong Kong. Although she hadn't wanted to work, Fanfan had to be independent and support herself after the divorce. She received a master's degree and worked as an accountant in California.

Ralph and I said goodbye to Fanfan and Young to continue our spring break. We walked on Hollywood Boulevard and saw in the distance the giant sign on the mountain; both were iconic. We also spent a whole day in Disneyland, a great treat. Growing up, I'd never had a similar fairytale place to visit. However, while being wowed at Disneyland, I also felt the economic constraints of not being able to enjoy it fully. *Someday, I will return and go on all the rides, visit every corner of it, and not worry about the cost.*

San Diego was our last stop before heading back. We had dinner at the home of one of Ralph's former classmates. The wife worked at a Chinese restaurant to support the husband's studies, a typical story of many Chinese couples in the U.S. Many years later, we learned from the media that the husband became a professor and had affairs with his students. The wife took him to court and eventually sent him to jail after revealing his illegal financial dealings. It was not typical among Chinese then that a wife would stand up in such a way and take revenge.

The driving was still the most thrilling of all my experiences on the spring break trip. Once back, I wanted to drive again and again. Ralph's car was not reliable. It was like a sick person, sometimes functioning but most of the time not. After being rejected by several garages, he tried to fix it, which proved ineffective. One day I hit a car while trying to park. White steam came out from the front and the car died. Ralph could not revive it.

I decided to get my own car and found a used Pontiac for $1400, a blue-gray hatchback with automatic transmission. Not crazy about the color, but I was glad it was an automatic transmission, thus easier to handle. The hatchback was extremely helpful—I was able to carry (on two separate trips) a monstrous 9-drawer chest and a dining table with chairs from a garage sale to my new apartment a few months later. That car was also responsible for transporting a friend from Las Cruces and me to Austin, TX. It hardly ever gave me any trouble.

Spring in Las Cruces was delightful, not too cold or hot. Ralph and I would go driving with or without a destination in mind.

We visited Yolanda's parents in Cloudcroft, where the daytime temperature allowed one to wear shorts and T-shirts, even while snowfall from previous nights remained on the ground. We drove to the White Sands area, where one's footprints in the snow-white sand would disappear almost as soon as they were made. We toured deserts and mountains in the surrounding areas—whatever was within a day's reach.

The freedom and empowerment I felt from driving were fascinating. I had so much choice—I could go anywhere, at any time. The best part was that I didn't have to be concerned with anything or anyone. For the first time in my life, I was authentically myself. I did not have to pretend, please, worry, or repress. I liked this new version of myself.

Three years later, I bought a newer and better car and sold my first car to a college freshman, who wrote the most extensive check of her life with a shaky hand for $1200.

Fig. 9.3. Standing in the snow. Cloudcroft, NM. 1990

Fig. 9.4. White Sands, NM. 1990

Fig. 9.5 Driving around with my first car. NM. 1990.

10

Movies and Music

I never quite figured out why Ralph's sore relationship with the rest of the local Chinese people got worse as time passed. Few of them spoke to him. Even his roommate got into a confrontation with him.

As the semester ended, many housing leases expired, and new ones had to be signed. Ralph and I decided to rent an apartment together for the summer. One day, while he was busy packing in his apartment, I cooked three dishes in my place and called him over for lunch. Just as he entered the door, his roommate Mr. Lin rushed in.

"Damn you! I haven't eaten for two days and am so stressed out. But look at you two. These many dishes! I'll let you eat! I'll let you eat!" Lin shouted. He lifted a dish and threw it on the floor. The plate broke into two pieces and the food splashed everywhere.

"What's the matter?" I was astonished.

Without answering me, Lin turned around, grabbed a cleaver knife from the counter, and started waving it before Ralph.

"Put that down." I calmly ordered and moved from the opposite side of the table to almost between them. I didn't believe he would use the knife.

The next thing I knew, Ralph had bolted out of my apartment and stood in the parking lot many yards away from the stairs facing our apartment. He was looking inside through the opened door.

Lin murmured something, put down the knife, and left.

I was dumbfounded—not by Lin's behavior but by Ralph's. *What if Lin had lost his mind and hurt me with the knife? Ralph ran for his life and didn't think about me at all.*

That was the first serious concern I had about Ralph.

He apologized later and explained that Lin had just gotten off the phone with his wife in China and his daughter had been ill. Lin was also struggling with his study.

"He isn't a sharp person at all," Ralph said.

I was too naive, and I forgave too quickly. But I didn't forget.

Another thing I couldn't forget was that Lin was kicked out of his Ph.D. program two days after the incident.

"Why?" I had the same question as many other Chinese students. All of us had moved mountains to get here—though different people had different kinds of mountains to move. This Ph.D. study was all I had, which was true for many other Chinese students.

"Told you, he is not a smart guy," Ralph said.

The reason for Lin's dismissal was kept a secret from everyone. He mysteriously disappeared. No one knew where he went. No one heard anything from him.

He left most of his stuff—though it wasn't much—at the apartment. So Ralph had to pack his things into a box and be the caretaker.

Ralph and I moved to a two-bedroom apartment for the summer, far from campus. The owners, Jack and Martha, an old childless couple, lived in the other apartment of the two-unit complex.

Jack was slim and tall. His shirts, whether T-shirts, polos, or short-sleeved buttoned shirts, would shift around his middle section. He moved smoothly and soundlessly as if not using his feet, often reminding me of a dragonfly. He had a full head of long gray hair that flowed in the air. His face was mostly clean, although I sometimes saw short sharp whiskers around his mouth. His eyes were large under the long, white eyebrows. I never asked about his age, but I guessed he was in his 60s or 70s.

"How is your day going?" Jack would ask from his chair under a big umbrella. He sat there a lot, sometimes reading newspapers, sometimes people-watching, though there wasn't much to watch since the house was at the end of a quiet street.

Martha was the opposite of Jack. She had round shoulders and a pear-shaped body. She would be considered short among the American women I had met. One always heard heavy footfalls before seeing her. Her eyes seemed completely shut when she smiled. Her short white hair was curly and neat, as if she just came back from the salon. She stayed inside a lot, mostly watching TV. "I can't stand the heat. My head burns," she would say.

One evening, Ralph and I joined them to enjoy one of the countless brilliant sunsets in Las Cruces.

"Why don't you move elsewhere?" I asked.

"What?" Jack was surprised by the question. "We've never thought about it. This is our hometown. We've never lived anywhere else," Jack said after thinking for a moment.

I looked at Martha, who brought out four cups of lemonade with a dinner tray.

"True. We like it here. Plus, our families are here. Our extended families," Martha said.

Jack started to list the whereabouts of their siblings, nephews, nieces, grand-nephews, and grandnieces. If any of them ever visited Jack and Martha, we must have missed them.

I could not imagine living my life in just one place, let alone a small town.

One Sunday morning, I went over to knock on their door.

"Jack and Martha, would you like to join us for dinner tonight? Ralph will cook pork belly and I'll make green beans and cabbage."

"Wonderful! We'll come. Would you like us to bring anything?" Jack was ecstatic. Martha grinned and nodded.

"No, no need to bring anything." Inviting people for dinner and expecting them to bring something was uncommon in China.

They brought red wine anyway. It was one of the most prolonged dinners I'd ever had at three hours.

"With school out for the summer, what are you kids doing?" Jack asked.

"My TA job is over, but I'm working 10 hours a week researching for my advisor," I answered.

"I'm free for three months. We're both looking for summer jobs," Ralph responded.

"Good luck finding jobs. What fun things do you do?" Jack asked.

"We've been catching up with movies, renting them from the Blockbuster next to Safeway," Ralph said.

"Any favorite actors?" Martha asked.

"Sly Stallone, Arnold Schwarzenegger, Bruce Willis," I said.

"We just watched *The Terminator* today," Ralph shared.

"Wow, you like action movies!" Jack raised his eyebrows.

"Action and sci-fi. Apple's favorites. Mine too," Ralph said.

"Before you came to this country, had you ever seen any movies made in the U.S.?" Martha asked.

"Yes. Several. The two I like the most are *Futureworld* and *First Blood*," I replied, excited.

After the Cultural Revolution ended in 1976, China opened the door—widely—to the rest of the world. That included importing many movies and adding Chinese voice-overs. In 1979, *Futureworld* was the first modern American movie to achieve a general theatrical release in China. It was initially shown inside various government organizations before being available to the public. My mom got two tickets and said, "Let's have a break from your college entry exam preparation."

Up to that point, the large auditorium that belonged to the provincial government had held countless political lectures, meetings, and cultural performances during festivals. But, that evening, excitement, expectations, uncertainty, and suspicion dominated the utterly full hall.

As the movie progressed, I became wholly absorbed by the story—humans were replaced by robots upon returning from a futuristic vacation location. There was not a single thing I could have anticipated. Turn after turn, surprise after surprise, my mind was catching up as fast as it could. It was not just the story unfamiliar to me but the concepts, logic, scenery, culture, norms, characters, clothing—everything. After watching it, I repeatedly played the movie back in my head. I questioned many instances and scenes, unsure if what I thought had happened was what did happen. I kept asking myself whether the two main characters were real humans when they returned. There seemed to be a clue to indicate the man was real. He seemed to have verified she was human after kissing her. But this innocent and peaceful look in the lady's eyes made me wonder if she could be so after struggling in fights, running, and escaping for her life. I repeatedly told myself that, for humanity's sake, let them be actual humans, not robots.

For a long time after that, my mind ran through many scenes, many what-ifs and maybes. I had nightmares about the guy from the West World chasing me. With no smile on his face and a sharp stare that pierced one's soul, he was so scary—and, at the same time, irresistibly handsome. When I saw a picture of people working in a factory in the newspaper, I imagined they were 300-level robots. Someone standing next to me might be a 500, or maybe even a 900 or 1100 level since they looked intelligent and genuine. *Futureworld* became hugely popular in China. Since watching that movie, I've loved science fiction stories, whether in films, TV shows, or books.

I heard about *First Blood* when I was home vacationing from graduate school in 1985. At that time, people could freely buy a ticket to a theater to watch a movie. My best friend from high school had come with me to see the film in a newly renovated and fully occupied movie theater. *First Blood* was said to be about a Vietnam War hero returning home, only to discover that he had to speak up for himself—via actions.

What an experience! An emotional rollercoaster! I hated the arrogant local officials and rooted for the wrongly treated war hero. What horrifying conditions and superb survival tactics. The well-trained special force skills. The iconic images and scenery. And Rambo! The humble, brave, rugged, muscular, and handsome Rambo, a man of few words but many actions.

First Blood was the first Hollywood blockbuster released in China. Word traveled quickly and far. Everyone I knew saw it, from the young generation to the old. The individualism philosophy and the heroic and rebellious nature of the movie might have tapped into many Chinese people's secret wishes. Chinese culture values collectivism and obedience. Growing up, we learned not to stand out from the crowd—the consequences were mostly negative—and not to challenge authorities, as it would be treated almost as a crime. Individuals did not count as much. As a result, we were used to a norm of not standing up for ourselves, not having our own opinions, not showing our uniqueness in any way, and just blending in with the crowd to survive. The end of China's Cultural Revolution and its wide-open position toward the world created a flux in many people's minds—though with great caution. A movie like this could have only been approved for showing under a ruler like Paramount Leader Deng Xiaoping, who led China from 1978 to 1989. Rambo might have acted on behalf of us all during that historical moment, despite his story happening in a faraway land and a completely different culture.

Although I knew *First Blood* was just a movie, I still considered it to reflect the reality of the U.S. It opened my eyes to America's perspective of the cruelty of the Vietnam War, which was still fresh in many Chinese people's memories when this movie was shown. We understood the war from the Party's news releases and propaganda. At times, war news dominated the radio. I was an elementary school student when the Vietnam War ended in 1975. We had to write about the war, the victory, and our love and appreciation for our troops who supported the Vietnamese. But whatever words came out were not really from our hearts but from what we had heard in the newspaper or on the radio.

From *First Blood*, I also learned about the potential injustice in America. *Unfortunately, there are stupid, arrogant, ignorant, and narrowly-minded people everywhere, including in the U.S. I wish there were more people like the Colonel in the movie.*

To my surprise, Jack and Martha had never seen either movie. They were fascinated by my stories, though.

"We should rent and watch them," Jack said to Martha. He then turned to us.

"About the Vietnam War—we saw *Apocalypse Now* and *The Deer Hunter*, which came out in the late 70s. *Platoon* came out later, I think, in the 1980s. Have you seen any of them?"

I remembered seeing *Platoon* right before I came to the U.S., although I could not recall many details apart from the fact that it was a war movie with lots of blood. There were many western movies available in China at that time. That might be why I did not remember it too clearly. *I should see it again and check out the two movies Jack mentioned so I'd know what they are about and understand more about how Jack, Martha, and other Americans see the Vietnam War.* I made a mental note to myself.

"Have you seen other Stallone movies?" Martha asked.

"Yes! We've watched *First Blood Part II*, *Rambo Part III*, and *Rocky I* through *Rocky IV*." Ralph showed his excitement about Stallone.

"We've also seen *Rocky I* and *Rocky II*. We loved them," Martha said.

We were momentarily silent as if everyone was ruminating on their Stallone favorites.

"Did you know any American musicians before you came?" Jack asked.

"Michael Jackson!" I answered without hesitation. Just the mention of his name brought up my heart rate.

In 1988, I put English preparation at the top of my priority list. It was the very first step in fulfilling my dream of studying abroad. Even though I had started learning English in middle school and continued to college, I needed to improve my proficiency to study overseas. As an international applicant, one must receive decent scores in the TOEFL (Test of English as a Foreign Language). I also signed up for a spoken English class to improve my conversational English.

One day, the instructor of spoken English showed us the MTV music video for Michael Jackson's song *Beat It*. The whole class of 20+ students was mesmerized. I held my breath while watching seemingly violent gangsters occupy the streets at night and worried that Michael's life was in danger. But, when Michael joined them and they started to dance together, I let out a long exhale and put my heart back where it belonged.

What a massive contrast to the types of music or entertainment we grew up with—revolutionary operas and political songs during 1966-1976, Teresa Teng's soft-toned pop music since 1980, Taiwanese folk songs since the mid-80s, among other comfortable pieces that could be enjoyed with eyes closed while sipping tea. Michael Jackson woke us up and touched all our senses and then some. We asked the instructor to play it again and again. How interesting the dance was! By the third time, many of us had started to move our heads, shoulders, arms, and legs along with the music in ways our parents might lecture us, "sit still when you're seated, don't jerk your body."

The instructor asked us, "How much did you understand the lyrics?"

"Two words: *beat it,*" one of us said, and we all laughed hard.

"Does it matter?" another asked, and everyone nodded, smiling.

"Yes—this is an English class, after all."

"But you are introducing American music to us. That matters more," another said.

"True. Do you want more?" The instructor teased us. He knew what our unanimous answer would be.

The highly anticipated next meeting finally came. We watched the music video *Thriller* multiple times. It was genuinely thrilling. The dance, the music, the plot, the goosebumps, the anticipations, the worries, the excitement, and the overall sensation. I became a diehard Michael Jackson fan.

11

SUMMER JOBS

Summer days felt longer than school days. I was excited by the prospect of trying different jobs to learn about the U.S. I also hoped to earn some much-needed money.

My first job was that of a salesperson. In the local newspaper, Ralph and I found an ad about selling air cleaning machines. The idea of clean air attracted me, and I wished there were such machines in China. However, I wondered how many Americans would spend thousands of dollars to buy such a machine, given that the air here was pretty clean already.

We attended multiple training sessions to learn how to demonstrate the machine and attract buyers. Our trainee group had seven people, all older than Ralph and me. Our manager/trainer, Joseph, was young, funny, and energetic. He always greeted us with ear-to-ear smiles, had jokes to make us laugh, was patient with each of us, and was enthusiastic about his job. Attending training sessions was generally pleasant, though we had road-blocks to clear with Joseph. I was the first to master how to disassemble and re-assemble the machine during the demo. But I had plenty of challenges. The script was written in a particular way. We had to speak the exact words in exact order, even though the order didn't always make sense to me. Reciting wasn't my strength. I preferred to understand the concept and tell the story my own way. I also had to practice my pronunciation, something no one else had to do. That took much of Joseph's time, and mine too at home.

"Congratulations! You all graduated from training!" Joseph high-fived each of us in our final training session.

"Now, you must rehearse what you learned with your family and friends. Here's a form to fill in their contact information. If any of them buy the machine during the rehearsal, you get 10% more than the cut you would get from a regular sale to a customer."

Some trainees were making noise that I could not understand.

"Don't worry. I'll go with you to each of your rehearsals. So you won't be doing it alone," Joseph said, seemingly responding to the stir among the trainees.

I raised my hand and asked: "What if we don't have families or friends?"

I didn't think any Chinese acquaintances would be interested since they could not afford it. I didn't feel comfortable approaching my American friends or colleagues either.

"You must have SOME friends?" Joseph raised one eyebrow, half teasing and half serious.

"Well, you know we are both international students." I pointed at Ralph and me.

"In that case, you can approach your neighbors or any neighborhood. Remember, these machines improve people's health and make their lives better. So you are doing an honorable thing by introducing the machines to people," Joseph said with a sincerity that showed he believed it.

"Do we get the same cut if we rehearse with neighbors?" Ralph asked.

"The 10% addition is just for family and friends. You get your usual 30% cut of the sale if you rehearse with strangers." Joseph was all business.

The other trainees seemed more cheerful.

Ralph and I drove around a few neighborhoods. We identified two that had larger houses and thus might be more prosperous than the others. We organized for Joseph to come with us on a Saturday afternoon.

I was glad to put on some of my fancier clothes and a pair of dress shoes, as there had been few opportunities to do so during the school year. At the first house, I rang the doorbell. A middle-aged man opened the door and looked at me with amazement as if he had never seen an Asian woman. I introduced myself and stated the purpose of the visit.

"What did you say you'll be doing?" he asked. My sentences were blurry to him.

"I would like to do a demo of this amazing air-cleaning machine. You have no obligation to buy it. However, it would be a great help to practice, and I'll thank you very much if you can give me the opportunity." I recited the script.

"Are they coming with you?" He looked over my shoulders at Ralph and Joseph, who were a few yards behind me.

"Yes, they help me with this big machine." That was outside the script.

"Sure, come on in." He opened the door wide and stepped aside.

Ralph rolled the machine in on its built-in cart. We stopped at the door to take off our shoes.

"Oh, you don't have to do that," the man said with a smile. Then he turned around and shouted, "Honey, we got visitors!"

A nice-looking lady came in from the other room. Following her was a young boy about 8 or 9 years old. Though she seemed slightly puzzled, her face showed a sincere welcome when I shook her hand after repeating what I would do. The boy immediately ran around Ralph who was disassembling the machine into several pieces.

As recommended in Joseph's training, I kept eye contact with homeowners instead of looking around the room. On the way in, I'd caught a glimpse—it was a lovely living room, but I could not see too much of it. I started to recite the script, picking up parts of the machine along the way and describing them. The demonstration should last no more than 20 minutes, but I had to repeat specific sentences. Despite that, from their facial expressions, I could tell that the couple did not get much of what I said. But they were polite and had encouraging smiles throughout the whole time.

"Good job," the man said after I finished.

"Sorry, my English is not very good," came out of my mouth uncontrollably.

"Your English is excellent. It must be hard to speak such a different language," the lady said.

I looked at Joseph, who nodded at me. I looked at Ralph, whose face told me I could have done better.

"You look lovely with that big smile. Keep it, and keep practicing," the man said when we waved goodbye to them. There was no sale.

We put the machine parts together and walked to the next house.

This time, Ralph rang the doorbell. The old lady had a broad grin after hearing what Ralph said and how he said it. That was the start of my realization that Ralph had a way with older ladies. He did a much better job with the presentation. He was animated, charming, and even cracked a joke or two—which was criticized later by Joseph, "stay with the script."

Again, no sale.

We did four more demos. Not a single sale. Fortunately, we were all welcomed into people's homes, and I got some good practice. As a result, I was much more confident in my later demos.

On Sunday afternoon, we drove to a different neighborhood. For some reason, half of the houses rejected us at the door, saying they were uninterested. As we approached the last home of the day, I felt the back of my feet hurting. I paused, took my shoe off, and saw blood on the back edge. *Too much walking in fancy shoes. But if we could get a sale, it'll all be worth it,* I reminded myself after finishing the last drop of water from my bottle. Another day with no sales.

At our next group meeting, one person reported selling a machine to his mom. Everyone cheered for him.

"Keep going. It'll get better. By the way," Joseph continued encouragingly, "Apple and Ralph are the hardest workers, and they did the most demos among you all."

I was thinking differently. I did some quick math. Ralph and I had done more than 20 demos in total. We estimated that the rest of the group might have done about the same number collectively. There had been only one sale after 40+ demos. That was not very promising. We decided to look elsewhere for a paying job.

Flipping through the newspaper, I saw an ad for a database administrator position with a new energy company. That would utilize skills that few other jobs do and that few people might have, thus giving me some advantage. I was excited and sent in my application. At the time, I did not know whether I could be legally employed or whether I could still stay in school to finish my degree if I were hired. I just wanted to go out there and give it a try. During the interview, I learned that this company utilized wind to generate energy. I asked why they didn't consider solar energy since New Mexico had an average of 360 sunny days per year. I was never called back after the interview.

Ralph and I realized being too picky about the jobs we sought was not a good idea. We'd try any jobs now to earn money. After calling a string of ads in the newspaper, we were called back to have an interview with Chem-Dry, a carpet cleaning company.

Mario greeted us with a gentle smile in his big dark eyes. He was Hispanic and had slightly dark skin and curly black hair that was neatly combed backward and fixed in place with gel. Just a little taller than Ralph, he was bulky, with biceps that screamed out of the short sleeves of his T-shirt.

"Think you can pick up that machine?" Mario pointed to a piece of equipment in the middle of the office. It was a cylinder with wheels and an extended U-shaped handler. It was smaller than the air cleaning machine we had trained with.

"Of course." Ralph went over to pick it up. He struggled.

"Much better if two people do it." Mario gestured to Ralph to go to one side, and together, they lifted the machine.

"Think you can control it when it's on?" Mario looked at Ralph with a smile.

"I'll see," Ralph said cautiously.

When the power was turned on, the machine started to dance in all directions. Ralph held onto the handle as hard as he could.

"Here, do it this way," Mario said, showing where to put his hands on the handle.

"You're hired," he nodded to Ralph. Then he turned to me.

"What would you like to do?"

"I can handle that machine as well." I stepped closer to the machine.

"Oh, no. I just needed one partner to do the job and I found him. Think you can answer phone calls and work in the office?"

"I'll give it a try." I had never done that kind of job. But staying in an air-conditioned office would be a nice treat in the hot summer.

"Did you say you are in Computer Science?"

"Yes, we both are," I nodded.

"My wife had someone build a database of customers, but it's not up to date. Think you can clean up the data and enter new customer contacts into it?"

"Yes, I can," I said, excited.

"Think you two can start tomorrow?" he asked.

Ralph and I looked at each other and said simultaneously, "Yes!"

"Ralph, you and I will go to houses; Apple, you'll stay until we return. There shouldn't be too many calls. You can work on that database the rest of the time. Think $5 per hour is acceptable?"

We had no idea if the rate was reasonable; we were just so happy to have the offer. We celebrated that evening.

Over the following three weeks, we'd arrive at the office at a time that was set the day before. Ralph and Mario would load that heavy machine into a van painted with a healthy, green grass theme and the big red words "Chem-Dry" on the sides. They'd visit between one and five houses during the day. I'd answer incoming calls. Sometimes, I had to ask the callers to repeat multiple times so that I could write the message down accurately. Well, maybe not as accurate as I would have wanted because I saw Mario raise his eyebrows sometimes when he called back customers.

Their database was poorly designed, with so many logic problems that I wondered how they could use it for anything. So, I decided to redesign it. My previous work experience in database design came in handy. It didn't take long for me to redo it. I then reloaded the existing records over to the new database. Finally, I started entering new customer records written on a stack of 3x5 index cards.

"You did what? Redesigned the database?" Mario was surprised when I proudly told him what I had done.

"The old one had a few errors that you could not get the right information out." I tried to explain my rationale but found it hard to communicate with him.

"My wife said it was good. She used it for a while," Mario said, displeased.

I didn't know what to say.

"Did you finish entering all the new customer records?"

"To the new database, yes, but not the old one."

"Think you can enter them into the old one?"

"Sure." I was not happy, but I knew I had to do it.

At home in the evenings, Ralph had been complaining about being sore since the second day of the job.

"I've never worked this hard my whole life," he grumbled.

"But you were raised in the countryside. So I'd think this would be no big deal to you," I said.

"I didn't have to work in the field if that's what you think. The hardest job I did was learning to build houses after high school. But that was skilled work, not hard labor."

He didn't have to suffer too much longer. By the end of the third week, Mario let us go.

Half of the summer had almost gone by at that point. The following job we got was doing yard work at a house. We only needed to visit once a week or as needed. Mowing the lawn, trimming the edges, and cleaning up whatever objects in the yard we were told to clean.

The pay rate was $5/hour too. The owner had a five-year-old girl who jumped around me and examined me from head to toe.

"Hi, I am Lucy. You're pretty," she said.

"You're prettier," I said back. It was true.

"I've never seen anyone like you."

"I've never played with a nice girl like you." That was also true. I disliked children, but she seemed cute and intelligent.

"Could you teach her Chinese?" her father asked me the second time we visited.

"Be glad to."

I liked the father's suggestion and looked forward to spending time with Lucy. But unfortunately, circumstances would cut the opportunity short, and I only got to teach her once.

12
MOVING ON

Just when I thought I'd be settled after the first semester and ready to start research under my advisor's supervision as part of my Ph.D. study, Dr. Davidson announced that he was moving to Tennessee in the fall of 1990 to be the chair of the Computer Science department. Now I was facing a decision about what was next for me. I also needed to secure financial aid for the next academic year and beyond.

My first plan was to stay and find another professor as my advisor. I checked with Professor Parry to see if he'd accept doctoral students.

"I don't do research. I'm a teaching professor," he told me.

That was the first time I'd heard of this kind of professor. No wonder he was teaching so many courses. Years later, I heard through the grapevine that Professor Parry left after his contract ended because the department wanted to replace him with someone with a Ph.D.

Since Professor Parry was out of the question, I looked around at the other research professors but did not see an obvious choice.

I must go somewhere else now. I'm back to the application stage again. But maybe I could build on what I've done so far. What about following Dr. Davidson to Tennessee? What about continuing the exploration with the University of Texas? Maybe I could approach these two options simultaneously just in case I run out of time and end up nowhere to be for the fall semester.

I brought up the idea of transferring to Tennessee to Dr. Davidson. He was delighted to hear it. He started the process immediately by searching for financial aid for me. By June 1990, he had secured a TA position for me in their CS department. However, ultimately the universe had different plans for me. That summer was the last time I saw Dr. Davidson. We would reconnect in 2002, twelve years later, after I had become a tenured professor. He had moved back to New Mexico by then and invited me to give a talk at a conference he had organized. I was eager to revisit Las Cruces, and the idea of a potential collaboration with him excited me. Months after we reconnected, I received a greeting card from his daughter Diana. She thanked me for keeping in touch with her father, sending him the newsletters I edited for a new professional community I'd established, and agreeing to give a talk at his conference. "Unfortunately, my father has passed away," she told me.

At the same time as asking Dr. Davidson to help me transfer to Tennessee, I found a letter from Dr. Wilson at the University of Texas at Austin in my suitcase. He had sent this letter to me in the summer of 1989 after I'd sent my Ph.D. application to him. The letter read as follows:

"Thank you for approaching me to be your advisor for the Ph.D. study. I like your computer science training and work experience in developing computer applications. It will be beneficial for studying in the business school. In addition, your academic publications can be used to substitute the required GRE test you don't have. I will forward your application to our admission committee."

The University of Texas had been the only other university I had heard from among the twenty-eight universities I had applied to. However, since NMSU's admission letter allowed me to leave China as soon as possible, I took that opportunity. Nevertheless, I still needed to follow up with Dr. Wilson.

I emailed him, recounting my short journey since our last conversation, and asked if it was still possible to be considered his Ph.D. student for fall 1990.

He immediately replied, "I remember you and am still interested. But our admission deadline has passed. If you want to try, you can meet with the admission committee and see what happens."

"Yes, I'll come and meet the committee." I was glad the door was not completely shut.

The 10-hour drive on I-10 was quite pleasant on a late April day. Ralph came with me and that made the trip more enjoyable. In addition, Dr. Wilson connected me with another Chinese doctoral student. She was very generous and let us stay in her apartment for free during the visit.

I was wowed by the six-story tall and shiny business school building. While the front side had light yellow bricks with tall and narrow windows, the main entry was almost two stories tall, wrapped in glass, including three double doors. One had to climb two flights of marble stairs from the street level to reach the main entrance. Upon entering the vast foyer, one was surrounded by walls filled with bronze-framed plaques of former leaders or donors. The dazzling sensation continued to the fifth floor, where Dr. Wilson's office was.

Dr. Wilson's 6'6" slim frame emerged from an inner room inside the office. He was in his mid-50s, had a full head of dark, curly hair, and a clean-shaven face. He walked toward us gently, and his big eyes behind a pair of oversized glasses seemed to take us all in.

He faced me and softly asked, "How was the trip?" He spoke slowly and clearly as if searching for the appropriate words and making sure the listener could understand him. His facial expression was calm.

"It was good." I could not find more words to say. Somehow, I was nervous.

"And you are?" he turned to Ralph.

"I'm Ralph," Ralph said and extended his right hand.

Dr. Wilson shook Ralph's hand lightly and said, "Nice to meet you."

He turned to me again. "The admission committee members are ready to meet you in about 30 minutes. The meeting room is 3-275. It is a bit tricky because of the way the rooms are numbered. I'll see you back here once you are done meeting them." With that, he returned to his inner room.

Dr. Wilson was right. It took us quite a while to figure out the numbering system of the building. Two admission committee members were already in the room when we arrived. Dr. Leighton was a Caucasian man with a large, tall frame, gray hair, and deep blue eyes. His face would shine pink when he was laughing or deeply engaged in a conversation, at which time his eyes would stare deeply into yours. Dr. Leighton had a cast on his left leg and moved his athletic body around on crutches. He was loud and teased a lot. Dr. Maddock was the opposite, skinny and short. Gray-haired too, Dr. Maddock had brown eyes that were almost covered by his long eyebrows. He didn't speak much, just asked a few questions quietly and avoided eye contact.

The meeting lasted about 40 minutes. There was laughter and easy-flowing conversation—kind of amazing because my

English was still not fluent. What I knew for sure was that I was not nervous, and I enjoyed the meeting.

"We have no problem recommending you. It is up to Dr. Wilson whether he could provide financial support," Dr. Leighton concluded. Dr. Maddock nodded in agreement.

I said thanks and goodbye to the two professors. Then, we went back to Dr. Wilson's office. I conveyed the committee's words to Dr. Wilson.

"I'll see what I can do," Dr. Wilson said quietly with his eyes on mine as if studying what I was thinking or what kind of a person I was. That made me nervous again.

I had done all I could do for the moment. So Ralph and I decided to drive around to enjoy the surroundings instead of returning to Las Cruces immediately.

We saw a sign on the highway for a natural cave and followed the directions to find a quiet entry inside some mountains. The cave was perfect for taking a break from the hot day. Stopping at a spot with no other visitors, I felt like I was in one of the caves in China during my travels to attend conferences. Nature was beautiful, regardless of whether in China or the U.S. I wanted to remember this cave and this visit. On the way out, I bought a tan short-sleeved shirt at the gift store with bright flowers on the front. It became one of my favorite tops.

At the end of June 1990, I was notified that I had been admitted to the Ph.D. program at the University of Texas. In addition, Dr. Wilson secured a TA position for me.

This was also when Dr. Davidson found a TA position for me in Tennessee. Between the two choices, I considered the Texas one more plausible because it would be in the academic field that I was inclined to do my Ph.D. study based on my experience in developing real-world computer applications in China. Moreover, half of my applications to American universities were for this field and half for computer science because I did not know whether this major would work out based on my background. In addition, the University of Texas was ranked higher and had a better reputation. Thus, it might be advantageous for my study and future job prospects. Nervously, I brought my decision to Dr. Davidson, hoping not to hurt him.

"You made the right choice to go to Texas. I'd do the same if I were you," Dr. Davidson assured me.

Studying in Texas would involve additional challenges. For example, I still needed to take courses in Business. Thus, I would have to make up for the necessary background I lacked. However, I was not afraid of taking classes. That should be fine and even exciting.

I quit my summer job teaching Chinese to five-year-old Lucy and got in the mode of moving. There were quite a few things to do, including finishing the summer research project with Dr. Davidson, completing all necessary paperwork for Texas, finding a roommate and an apartment, and registering for courses for the fall semester.

Ralph and I started to have arguments in July. Both being stubborn, we had cold wars that could last for days.

To prepare for my drive to Austin, I went to the AAA office to request a booklet of maps.

"Is the car still under your name?" the lady at the counter asked after checking my AAA card and looking into her computer.

"Yes. Why?" The car had been under my name since I bought it. I did add Ralph as another authorized driver at that time.

"Someone called a few days ago and canceled the car's insurance. Is that your boyfriend?"

"Was."

"Oh. I'm so sorry to hear that. Would you like to buy it now?" The lady looked at me with great sympathy. I pulled out my checkbook and wrote the amount needed to cover the cost.

Driving a car without insurance would be against the law and could result in jail time. Ralph had told me that long ago. Yet, he had canceled mine without notifying me, and I had been driving without it for the past several days. I would have gone to Texas without it, too.

I hadn't realized he hated me so much that he would do such a nasty thing to me. Actually, I should not have been surprised by that. There had been a few instances already. For example, a couple of weeks prior, we had decided to order a pizza for dinner.

"I'm going to order and pick it up," Ralph said.

"No onion, please." I liked pizzas but hated onions on top.

He came back shortly with a pizza that had onions on it.

"Why onions?"

"They wouldn't customize the order," he said without looking at me.

It was a blatant lie because I had learned that every customer could customize the toppings by then—what if someone had an allergy?

"Such a liar you are!"

"I'm not. You can go and ask." He did not meet my eyes.

"You don't care about me, do you?"

"You are not the only one who's important."

"Of course not. You just demonstrated it again. No wonder your wife left you."

"You keep her out of this!" His voice raised and his face grew red.

"Why should I? You deserve what you got. And you deserve to be single!"

I was so upset that I left our apartment for several hours to cool down. The next day, I found that our joint bank account balance was now less than $100 with $800 missing. When I confronted him about it, he said his friend had needed money and he'd lent the $800 to him. Again, I felt sick about his behavior and yet another lie.

A few days before leaving for Texas, we had another big argument. I'd been hoping to be his Jane Eyre, to fall in love and stay with the first man who swept me off my feet. However, signs gradually revealed that Ralph was not my Mr. Rochester. Ralph's only similarity to Mr. Rochester was that he'd been married before. The differences between us were too huge, and the tender, loving feeling we once had was disappearing.

The decision to break up with him was not easy. He was my first love, owning my first kiss and first night. Yet I did not feel he valued me and did not care for or love me the way I thought a boyfriend should. Finally, I convinced myself that breaking free from him was the right thing to do. At the same time, my heart was bleeding.

Driving down southeast on I-10 again, but this time alone, my mood gradually lifted as the scenery improved. Trees were greener and taller, buildings grander and more spread out, and traffic much heavier. The sky seemed higher, too. There was a sense of abundant opportunities and excitement.

What is waiting for me in Austin? Will it be like Las Cruces? In what ways? Is it easier for me now that I'm familiar with some cultures and norms? Will I continue to meet kind and generous people? Will I succeed in getting my Ph.D.? Will I be able to find an academic job to continue my childhood dream of being a professor? Will I be able to stay in this new country that has welcomed me already? Will I find love again?

I couldn't wait to start my life in Texas!

~~~ To be Continued ~~~

13
Dear Reader

If you enjoyed this book, please consider leaving a review at Amazon or Goodreads so that other readers will know if this is a book they will enjoy.

If you would like to read more of Apple's life stories, please sign up her newsletter at https://subscribepage.io/eBLuxe or with the following QR code. Upon signing up, you will receive a free piece related to her upcoming books.

APPLE AN

Thank you!

14

About the Author

Apple An (pen name) grew up during China's Cultural Revolution. She came to the U.S. in her 20s, earned a P h.D., and is a professor at Syracuse University, Syracuse, New York. She considers her greatest accomplishment to be raising three successful children and being the guardian of her beautiful nephew and niece. She writes about her life and the lives of people she knows. Her short stories appear in various places, including *Fiveminutelit*, and *fauxomir lit mag*, among others. She hopes her writings enrich Asian American cultural heritage and history, thus enhancing cultural understanding and acceptance among all people.

www.AppleAnBooks.com

www.ingramcontent.com/pod-product-compliance
Lightning Source LLC
Chambersburg PA
CBHW020312010526
44107CB00001B/72

9 781958 900055